SMOOTHIE-LICIOUS

Power-Packed
Smoothies and
Juices
the Whole Family
Will Love

Jenna Helwig

Copyright © 2015 by Jenna Helwig

Photography © 2015 by Lauren Volo

Designed by Alissa Faden

For information about permission to reproduce
selections from this book, write to Permissions,
Houghton Mifflin Harcourt Publishing Company,
215 Park Avenue South, New York, New York 10003.

www.hmhco.com

Library of Congress Cataloging-in-Publication Data is
available.

ISBN 978-0-544-37008-1 (pbk); ISBN 978-0-544-
50573-5 (ebk)

Printed in the United States of America

DOC 10 9 8 7 6 5 4 3 2 1

To Dave: Thank goodness for mergers

TABLE OF CONTENTS

INTRODUCTION

As a mom, I know that parents want to feed their children well. We want to give our kids a protein-packed breakfast before school and a healthy snack when they get off the bus in the afternoons. We would love to incorporate more whole foods into our families' diets—if only there were an easy, foolproof way of eating that we knew our kids would love.

I am here to tell you that a solution exists, an answer so easy and healthy it's almost magic. That solution, of course, is the smoothie.

Not many kids will be choosy about a sweet, creamy, cold drink, regardless of the ingredients. Smoothies come together in five minutes or less and require approximately zero cooking skills to blend up. They may just be the perfect food for children.

But that doesn't mean that smoothies are just kid stuff. We adults need protein, fiber, healthy fats, vitamins, and minerals just as much as our kids. And as movie stars and fitness gurus will attest, produce-rich smoothies are a fantastic way to up the nutritional ante of a meal. The fact that all of this good stuff can be blended into a crave-worthy beverage is just the icing on the cake (so to speak).

Let's face it, smoothies are *fun*. In creating smoothies, you are only limited by your imagination, and that's where this book comes in. *Smoothie-licious* features 75 healthy, delicious recipes for smoothies and whole fruit juices—none of which contain refined sugars (well, just

one, but it's optional), only a little honey, pure maple syrup, or agave if the recipe needs a bit of sweetening. Because entire fruits and vegetables are blended, and not merely pressed for their juice, the resulting beverages are packed with antioxidants, vitamins, minerals, and fiber, which is lacking in most juices and contributes to satiety and digestive health. The addition of seeds, yogurt, and nut butters provides protein and other essential nutrients. And best of all, each of these recipes can be prepared with a common blender, no expensive professional-grade blenders or juicers required.

My conversion to smoothies as a family-friendly power food is relatively recent. When I was a kid growing up in the suburbs of Denver, my mother would make a homemade "Orange Julius" on special occasions such as my birthday or Christmas. It was made with milk, frozen orange juice concentrate, water, sugar, and ice. Cold, thick, and creamy, it separated if you didn't

★ SUPERSTAR ATTRIBUTES ★

FROM START TO FINISH, MOST SMOOTHIES DON'T TAKE MORE THAN FIVE MINUTES TO PREPARE.

ALL MANNER OF FRUITS AND VEGETABLES CAN BE BLENDED IN.
Better yet, you can choose to highlight their flavors or, um, mask them, depending on the audience for your culinary creations.

A SMOOTHIE CAN BE A VEHICLE FOR ALL SORTS OF PROTEINS —
Greek yogurt, nut butters, chia seeds, and hemp seeds, to name a few.

SMOOTHIES ARE PORTABLE.
Pour them in a thermos and head off to school or work for an easy breakfast on the go.

BECAUSE YOU'RE BLENDING SWEET, NATURAL FRUIT, YOU'LL LIKELY NEED LITTLE IF ANY ADDED SWEETENER.

SMOOTHIES ARE PERFECT FOR BREAKFAST, SNACK TIME, LUNCH, OR DESSERT.
They are also delicious frozen in ice pop molds (as you'll see) or served in small glasses at a party.

KIDS CAN PARTICIPATE TOO.
While bringing kids into the kitchen can seem like asking for trouble (or at least a big mess to clean up), they can't do much damage with a smoothie. Put ingredients in the blender and push the button. Just remember to put the top on first.

SMOOTHIES GENEROUSLY INCORPORATE THE ODDS AND ENDS OF YOUR CRISPER AND FRUIT BOWL.
Have half a banana, a handful of spinach, and a plump date? Bingo, smoothie time. This flexibility also makes smoothies budget-friendly.

NATURALLY VEGETARIAN, SMOOTHIES ARE ALSO EASY TO MAKE VEGAN.
Simply swap out cow's milk and nix any honey in the recipe. And since they contain no wheat, most are also gluten-free. (A few of the smoothies include oats; be sure to buy gluten-free oats if you're on a wheat-free diet.)

NO COOKING REQUIRED!

REMINISCENT OF A MILKSHAKE
Thanks perhaps to their close resemblance to their cousin the milkshake, smoothies are generally regarded as treats, no matter how healthy they are. After all, everyone likes to sip something cool and creamy through a straw. We parents can use this to our advantage.

drink it fast enough. But that wasn't usually a problem. The sweet drink was a highlight of any holiday breakfast.

As I grew up, smoothies were always a special occasion treat. Even as a teenager, it never occurred to me that I could blend up a smoothie any old time. (In fact, smoothies are a perfect food for teenagers to make for themselves!)

As an adult I occasionally whipped up a plain-Jane smoothie with a banana, milk, and ice. It wasn't until I participated in a 10-day "detox" that I realized all that smoothies had to offer, especially where kids are concerned. During this period I cut out caffeine (eek!), alcohol, sugar, gluten, and dairy. I strove to incorporate vegetables into every meal, and in doing so realized that smoothies were the perfect way to veggify my breakfasts. Not only could I blend up all sorts of nourishing foods, but with a few smart additions I could ensure they were absolutely delicious and satisfying. My culinary *pièce de résistance* was a thick, creamy concoction of coconut milk, avocado, spinach, and frozen mango chunks. Morning after morning I happily sipped away at this subtly sweet and almost decadently smooth drink. I was hooked.

But what really caught my attention is what happened next.

Unsurprisingly, my then-six-year-old daughter, Rosa, wanted in on the fun. It looked like I was having a milkshake for breakfast, after all. But, picky kid alert: Rosa detests avocados. (She has declared that the worst foods in the world are a tie between asparagus and avocado.) Nevertheless, I gave her a sip of my smoothie and held my breath. She promptly asked for her own glass.

Since I am not one of those moms who generally believe in "hiding" foods from children, I reluctantly disclosed the smoothie's ingredients. Rosa was surprised, but undeterred. After all, you can't argue with yummy. This celadon-green smoothie (Avocado Bliss on page 54) is still one of her favorite breakfasts or snacks frozen in ice pop molds.

Since then, our ingredient repertoire has expanded to include dates, frozen grapes, frozen strawberries, blueberries, apples, cucumber, chia seeds, kale, flaxseeds, almond milk, Greek yogurt, acai, peaches, pomegranate juice, and more. And I blend up a smoothie nearly every day of the week.

The recipes in *Smoothie-licious* are our family's favorites. They have been served at breakfast, brunch, lunch, after school, at play-dates, and as dessert. The smoothies are fast, easy, healthy, and delicious, and I'm excited to share them with you.

A Touch of Sweet

Veg

Boost

Frost

THE ANATOMY OF A SMOOTHIE

FOR A SATISFYING SMOOTHIE YOU NEED A FEW KEY COMPONENTS.

HERE ARE MY FAVORITE BUILDING BLOCKS, ALONG WITH EQUIPMENT ADVICE AND NUTRITIONAL INFORMATION.

Not every recipe calls for an ingredient from each of these groups, but knowing a smoothie's basic elements will help you customize your drinks and create your own recipes down the road.

The Base This is the liquid in the smoothie, and for creaminess and flavor, is usually some type of milk. These days with the proliferation of non-dairy milks the options can seem never-ending. Some of the most popular are cow, almond, coconut, rice, and soy milks. In this book, these milks are virtually interchangeable, especially when blended with flavorful fruits. Choose the one (or two or three) you prefer based on your family's nutritional needs and tastes.

That said, I have three go-to milks for smoothies. The first is unsweetened almond milk. To me, this milk is a blank canvas flavor-wise. Plus, it's sugar-free, a big bonus since we're typically adding lots of naturally sweet fruits to these drinks. Almond milk can be found boxed on the shelf or in a carton in the refrigerated section. When you're shopping for almond milk, make sure to check the ingredient label and choose a variety with no added sugar.

Another great smoothie base is coconut milk. Lower in total sugar than cow's milk, it has a creamy, tropical flavor that I adore. Be sure to buy coconut milk beverage in cartons, as opposed to concentrated canned coconut milk, which is significantly higher in fat and calories. You should be able to find it in most grocery stores either in the refrigerated section with the soymilk or with the shelf-stable almond milk. My favorite brands are Silk Coconutmilk, Coconut Dream, and So Delicious.

Finally, I sometimes call for cow's milk for its classic taste. We drink 2 percent milk at my house, but keep in mind that children under age two should drink full-fat milk (and eat full-fat yogurt) to meet their daily fat requirements necessary for brain development. Cow's milk is also higher in protein than plant-based milks, so if you want to augment a smoothie's protein power, sub in cow's milk for almond or coconut.

Again, these recipes truly will work with any milk you choose. And, while milks are the main source of liquid in these smoothies, I do rely on a limited quantity of pomegranate juice, orange juice, coconut water, and good old H_2O.

The Fruit From succulent mangos to bright-tasting raspberries to more understated apples, it's no surprise that fruit is at the heart of most smoothies. Not only are they delicious, they are packed with fiber, vitamins, and minerals. So fresh fruits abound in this book, and sweet and sticky dried fruits like dates and figs also make an appearance, adding a concentrated sweetness. These smoothies showcase my family's favorite fruity combinations, but feel free to make substitutions, strawberries for raspberries, say, based on your tastes and your refrigerator's contents. In general, use the ripest fruit you have; you'll be rewarded with a sweet, bright flavor. A quick prep tip: Unless otherwise noted, there's no need to peel apples, pears, or peaches. You'll save a few minutes and score an additional boost of fiber.

The Velvet Smoothies don't need to be creamy. They can be refreshing and delicious when a little slushier. But I can't lie: I love the milkshake-like quality a good smoothie can offer. Bananas—frozen or not—are stellar at providing that creamy texture, so you'll see them in many of these recipes. Avocados, too, make for a delectably smooth sip. Yogurt, soaked chia seeds, and silken tofu can also add a luscious, velvety texture.

HOMEMADE ALMOND MILK

If you're keen to DIY, almond milk is surprisingly simple to make at home. Start by soaking 1 cup of raw almonds in water overnight. Drain and place the almonds in the blender with 4 cups of fresh water, a pinch of salt, and a squeeze of agave (optional). Blend until smooth. Place a fine-mesh strainer over a pitcher or bowl, line it with cheesecloth, and pour the contents of the blender into the strainer. With a ladle or wooden spoon, push down on the solids in the strainer to extract as much almond milk as possible. Discard (or compost) the solids. (Another option is to use a nut milk bag in place of the sieve. Available online for less than $10, a nut milk bag makes for an even silkier milk since less of the solids make it into the final product.) You'll get 3 to 4 cups of milk. Store your milk in the fridge for up to four days. And, don't stop with almond milk. This recipe works with virtually any nut, including walnuts and cashews.

Cow's Milk

The Frost To give a smoothie that cool, shake-like quality, we need to incorporate an icy ingredient. This could be, well, ice of course. But I prefer to work with frozen fruit for a few reasons. As ice melts it waters down the smoothie. It doesn't add any flavor, and no matter how much you blend it seems that there are always unpalatable chunks of ice remaining. Instead, I favor banana slices, grapes, or pineapple chunks that I freeze ahead of time in zip-top bags, or store-bought frozen berries, cherries, mango chunks, acai, cranberries, or peaches. In addition to being convenient, bagged frozen fruit is also economical, nutritious, and often just as flavorful as its fresh counterparts, especially when a fruit is out of season.

A FRUIT-FULL FREEZER

To make any smoothie you like on the spur of the moment, it's smart to keep already prepped fruit in the freezer. Stock up on bagged frozen fruit at the grocery store, and whenever you have bananas on hand make it a habit to save a couple of ripe ones for the freezer. Peel, slice, and bag each individual banana in a small zip-top bag, since most recipes call for a single banana. And go beyond bananas. At my house, we often have grapes or pineapple chunks languishing in the fridge, almost, but not quite, past their prime. Into the freezer they go, and then I'm ready to blend up a smoothie without any advance prep.

Peanut Butter

Yogurt

Silken Tofu

Coconut Water

For the best smoothie texture, stick with either fresh or frozen fruit depending on what the recipe calls for. If you do substitute frozen strawberries for fresh, for example, be prepared to add a bit more liquid since your smoothie will be extra icy. Conversely, if you swap in fresh mango for frozen, say, your smoothie will be significantly thinner and less creamy.

The Veg
Here is the ingredient that makes smoothies so versatile. A handful of kale, a smidgen of spinach, or a few chunks of cucumber go a long way to add nutritional power to your drink. Naturally sweet vegetables like beets, carrots, and sweet potatoes also take star turns. My hands-down favorites are avocados for their aforementioned creamy quality and pre-washed baby spinach for its convenience and mild taste.

The Boost
Peanut butter, almond butter, or another nut butters add both flavor and a punch of protein to a smoothie. Feel free to sub in one for another, or use sunflower butter if there is a nut allergy in your household. I prefer to work with unsweetened (and unsalted) nut butters, so I can control the sweetness of my smoothie. Yogurt and silken tofu also add protein and body to some of the drinks.

To up a smoothie's nutritional ante even more, many recipes call for those nutrition superheroes—seeds. Flaxseeds boast fiber, omega-3s, and beneficial lignans, which may reduce the risk of cancer. Hemp seeds are a rich source of protein; chia seeds offer fiber and omega-3 fatty acids. If soaked for 10 minutes first, chia seeds also turn gelatin-like, naturally thickening the drink. But we don't need to stop at seeds. Whole nuts add protein and texture; oats contribute a toasty flavor, plus loads of fiber.

The Flavor Kick
Maybe it's vanilla or almond extract, a teaspoon of cocoa powder, or a sprinkle of cinnamon—a dash of concentrated flavor can take a ho-hum smoothie to hip hip hooray.

A Touch of Sweet
Thanks to naturally sweet fruits, many of the recipes in this book call for no additional sweetener. Some of the smoothies though, especially those with a higher proportion of vegetables, do call for a teaspoon or two of agave, honey, or maple syrup. But most of the recipes in *Smoothie-licious* include sweetener as an option. In those cases I encourage you to prepare the smoothie as directed and then take a quick taste before deciding whether to add some sweetness. This is especially important since the flavor of each individual smoothie will vary based on the ripeness of the fruit. Sometimes a strawberry smoothie made with out of season berries will need a shot of agave. The same drink made with fresh, ripe, local strawberries might be blissfully sweet with no help at all.

I like giving kids the job of deciding if a smoothie needs more sweetness. Ask your child to taste test first before adding the sweetener. This gives kids a sense of ownership in the beverage and makes it even more likely that they'll drink up. Don't be afraid to add a little sweetener if your kids request it. A half teaspoon of honey is a small price to pay to make particular smoothies more palatable to tough customers in your family.

None of the recipes (well, one) call for refined sugars such as granulated white or standard brown sugars. Instead, I reach for agave nectar, maple syrup, or honey. In addition to the fact that these sweeteners contain trace nutrients, I like the fact that they're already in convenient liquid form, perfect for blending into a smoothie or juice. Agave is the sweetener you'll see most often simply because I appreciate its neutral flavor. Maple syrup is another favorite for its deep, caramel undertones. Be sure to buy a pure maple syrup with no additional ingredients. I prefer a darker variety, but any type will do. I use honey more sparingly simply because its flavor is quite distinct. But feel free to employ these sweeteners interchangeably based on your family's tastes and what you have on hand.

Honey

Maple Syrup

Agave Nectar

FOOLPROOF FORMULA
for a
LIP-SMACKING SMOOTHIE

BASE

+

FRUIT

+

VELVET

+

FROST

+

(VEG, BOOST, & A TOUCH OF SWEET)

=

SCRUMPTIOUS

THE GOOD-FOR-YOU STUFF

Each recipe in this book features nutritional information, so you can get a sense of how much fiber, Vitamin C, calcium, and other important nutrients are in each drink. I've also flagged any nutrients that meet 15 percent or more of an adult's recommended daily allowance; they meet an even higher percentage of a child's nutritional requirements.

Plus, certain recipes are marked with symbols so you can easily identify their nutritional qualities:

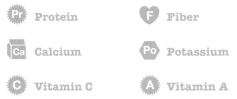

Meal-in-a-Glass: A smoothie with this symbol has enough calories, protein, and fiber to stand in for a child's breakfast, lunch, or hearty, nutritionally balanced snack.

Gluten-free: The vast majority of recipes in this book are gluten-free. To make recipes containing oats gluten-free, look for gluten-free oats such as Bob's Red Mill.

Vegan: No animal products in sight in these recipes, including cow's milk, yogurt, or honey.

Pr	Protein	F	Fiber
Ca	Calcium	Po	Potassium
C	Vitamin C	A	Vitamin A

These symbols highlight smoothies that are good sources of essential nutrients, crucial for keeping both kids and adults healthy and strong.

The smoothie recipes in *Smoothie-licious* make two approximately 12 oz. smoothies. The recipes for whole fruit juices make two 8 oz. juices. Since you may be blending for just one, more than two, or for adults who crave a larger drink, know that it's easy to adjust your final quantity. Most of the recipes are simple to halve, increase by 50 percent, or even double.

EQUIPMENT

One of the best qualities of the smoothies and juices in *Smoothie-licious* is that they don't require any specialized equipment. While of course a high-powered, professional blender will do the job (and then some), all of these recipes were tested with a standard, five-speed blender, specifically a KitchenAid. The only other equipment required is liquid measuring cups (a 2-cup measure is sufficient), dry measuring cups, standard measuring spoons, and a fine-mesh sieve for straining out berry seeds in the whole fruit juice recipes.

STORING

While smoothies will taste freshest immediately after blending and are easy to pour into a travel mug for sipping in transit, they can certainly be made ahead. Simply blend them up the night before, store in a covered cup, and take it from the fridge as you walk out the door. Just give it a shake before drinking. And, remember that smoothies thicken in the refrigerator, so consider adding more liquid if preparing ahead. One option I recommend if it's feasible: Place the non-frozen ingredients in the blender the night before (be sure to submerge avocados, bananas, pears, and apples in the liquid so they don't brown) and refrigerate. In the morning, add the frozen fruit and blend away. This way you'll have saved a few minutes of measuring during the morning rush, but the smoothie will still taste creamy and fresh.

FREEZE IT

As if sipping a smoothie isn't fun enough, virtually every recipe in this book also makes a stellar ice pop. The method couldn't be simpler. Pour a blended smoothie into ice pop molds and freeze until solid. Voilà! You have an easy, healthy, kid-friendly treat, perfect for hot summer days or really any time of the year. If you don't have ice pop molds fill small paper cups ¾ of the way full. Once the smoothie is partially frozen, in about 45 minutes, slide a craft stick into the center of each cup, and freeze until solid.

FRUIT-FILLED

1

Nature's Candy

Berry, Berry Healthy

Smoothie VIP

Liquid Sunshine

WHEN MOST PEOPLE THINK "SMOOTHIE,"

creamy concoctions bursting with healthy, sweet fruit come to mind. The smoothies in this chapter range from the perfectly simple, with just a few ingredients, to the deliciously complex, with a blend of fruits and other flavors. Choosier eaters might find the drinks in this chapter the most palatable, and who could blame them? These smoothies are packed with pineapple, mango, raspberries, apples, and other vibrant-tasting (and fiber-rich) fruits. Feel free to experiment with flavors, swapping one fruit for the other or substituting a different variety of milk. For the best texture, be sure to maintain the ratio between fresh and frozen ingredients. Also, keep in mind that fruits differ in size. For example, many recipes call for one banana. If the banana you're using is particularly large or small, be prepared to adjust the quantity of the liquids you're using. Here are the fruits on my smoothie shortlist:

Bananas Ladies and gentlemen, behold the most miraculous fruit in the smoothie world: the all-powerful banana. Healthy? Without a doubt. Everyone knows that bananas are a good source of potassium, but they are also loaded with fiber, Vitamin C, Vitamin B_6, and manganese. Better still, in addition to their natural sweetness, which only gets more pronounced as they ripen, they contain a tiny bit of healthy fat, which makes the resulting smoothie creamy and delicious—especially if you use a frozen banana. As far as I'm concerned, my freezer isn't complete without at least three peeled, sliced, and frozen bananas inside waiting for my next spark of smoothie inspiration.

Berries Strawberries, raspberries, blackberries, and blueberries are the jewels of the fruit world, jam-packed with antioxidants and boasting a reliably kid-friendly taste. In terms of consumption, strawberries are the most popular member of the berry family, but they come with a hitch. Out of season strawberries are notoriously disappointing—gorgeous, but all too often flavorless. Most of the year I stick with frozen, then come May, June, and July I go crazy with strawberries from the farmers' market. I find that blueberries, raspberries, and blackberries taste okay in the winter months, but they are just as sweet (and less expensive) in their frozen form.

Tropical Fruits Mango and pineapple—whether fresh or frozen—add a burst of sunny flavor, a pretty bright color, and a healthy dose of Vitamin C to any smoothie or whole food juice. When blending a fresh mango, be sure to pick a ripe one; either the common Tommy Atkins variety or a creamy-fleshed champagne mango, also called an Ataulfo, if you can find it. Pineapple is another natural smoothie ingredient and one that makes me feel especially thrifty, since my family can rarely eat an entire pineapple before it goes bad. Now I chop half to eat fresh and freeze the rest for smoothies.

Cherries While I love fresh cherries, their season is short and, let's face it, pitting them is kind of a pain. Nope, I'll stick with eating fresh cherries out of hand in July and blend up sweet frozen (pre-pitted!) cherries in my smoothies the rest of the year. Less overtly sugary than many other fruits, cherries have a deep, lush taste that pairs well with chocolate. They also blend up more creamy than icy, a rarity when it comes to frozen fruit.

Apples When I first started concocting smoothies, apples weren't the first fruit I thought of, or even in the top 10, really. But as I began expanding my smoothie horizons I realized that I was giving apples short shrift. Their familiar, comforting taste plays so well with nut butters and other more substantial ingredients, the fact that they are a good source of fiber and blood sugar regulating polyphenols is almost beside the point. Stick with whole apples as opposed to apple juice whenever possible. They blend up well and you'll get their all-important fiber instead of just a sugar rush.

Dates A brilliant source of natural sugars, dates are a healthful way to satisfy a sweet tooth. Look for Medjool dates, sometimes found in a grocery store's produce section. Larger than the bagged dates I grew up with, they should be soft, wrinkly, and easy to pit with your fingers. A good source of potassium and magnesium, dates will add a concentrated sweetness to any smoothie, along with a caramel taste that makes me swoon. If your dates are especially leathery, pit them and soak them in warm water for 10 minutes before blending.

RASPBERRY-ORANGE PUNCH

Makes 2 smoothies

I'm not sure which is brighter—this smoothie's flavor or its hot pink hue. Perfect with breakfast, lunch, or as a light snack, this is one punch the whole family will welcome.

½ CUP COCONUT WATER

½ CUP ORANGE JUICE

1 CUP SLICED STRAWBERRIES

1 BANANA

1 CUP FROZEN RASPBERRIES

1 Add all of the ingredients to the blender, starting with the liquids.

2 Cover and blend until smooth, about 30 seconds.

Nutrition per serving: 156 calories; 3g protein; 1g fat (0g sat. fat); 38g carbohydrates; 8g fiber; 21g sugars; 66mg sodium; 47mg calcium; 1mg iron; 607mg potassium; 80mg Vitamin C; 95IU Vitamin A

MANGO MADNESS

Makes 2 smoothies

Just four ingredients and a blender will transport you to the tropical locale of your dreams. Thanks to plump dates and protein-rich Greek yogurt, this smoothie is creamy and lush, with an almost caramelized sweetness. And if you happen to be drinking this smoothie sans kiddos, go ahead and add a drop of rum. I won't tell.

1½ CUPS COCONUT MILK

½ CUP PLAIN GREEK YOGURT

4 DATES, PREFERABLY MEDJOOL, PITTED

1½ CUPS FROZEN MANGO CHUNKS

1. Add all of the ingredients to the blender, starting with the coconut milk.

2. Cover and blend until smooth, about 30 seconds.

Nutrition per serving: 346 calories; 6g protein; 11g fat (5g sat. fat); 63g carbohydrates; 7g fiber; 54g sugars; 65mg sodium; 148mg calcium; 2mg iron; 609mg potassium; 62mg Vitamin C; 3217IU Vitamin A

PEAR-FECT APPLE SMOOTHIE

Makes 2 smoothies

A shoo-in at breakfast, this smoothie also makes a great afterschool snack, preferably in the fall when apples, pears, and grapes are all in season. It's crisp and creamy at the same time, perfect sipped through a straw to tide kids over until dinner.

1 CUP MILK

1¼ CUPS CHOPPED APPLE (ABOUT 1 MEDIUM)

1 CUP CHOPPED RIPE PEARS
(OR USE CANNED PEARS)

¾ CUP FROZEN GRAPES

2 LARGE GRAHAM CRACKER RECTANGLES,
OPTIONAL

HONEY TO TASTE, OPTIONAL

1. Add the milk, apple, pears, and grapes to a blender.

2. Cover and blend until smooth, about 30 seconds.

3. If using the graham crackers, break into pieces and add to the blender. Blend until smooth.

4. Taste for sweetness, adding honey if desired.

Nutrition per serving: 172 calories; 5g protein; 3g fat (2g sat. fat); 35g carbohydrates; 5g fiber; 22g sugars; 64mg sodium; 168mg calcium; 0mg iron; 436mg potassium; 10mg Vitamin C; 349IU Vitamin A

MEXICAN FROZEN HOT CHOCOLATE

Makes 2 smoothies

This lightly spiced smoothie may taste like dessert,
but it's healthy enough for a nutritious snack.

1½ CUPS COCONUT MILK

2 BANANAS, SLICED AND FROZEN

4 TEASPOONS UNSWEETENED
COCOA POWDER

1 TEASPOON VANILLA EXTRACT

½ TEASPOON GROUND CINNAMON

1 PINCH CHILI POWDER

1 PINCH SALT

1. Add all of the ingredients to the blender, starting with the coconut milk.

2. Cover and blend until smooth, about 30 seconds.

Nutrition per serving: 170 calories; 2g protein; 4g fat (3g sat. fat); 37g carbohydrates; 6g fiber; 20g sugars; 90mg sodium; 105mg calcium; 2mg iron; 552mg potassium; 10mg Vitamin C; 456IU Vitamin A

BANANAS FOR STRAWBERRY-KIWI

Makes 2 smoothies

This classic combination will appeal to kids with more
traditional (read: cautious) palates. None of the flavors are tart
or overpowering, just light and sweet.

1 CUP COCONUT MILK

1 BANANA

2 KIWIS, PEELED AND CHOPPED

1 CUP FROZEN STRAWBERRIES

AGAVE NECTAR, OPTIONAL

1. Add the coconut milk, banana, kiwis, and strawberries to the blender, starting with the coconut milk.

2. Cover and blend until smooth, about 30 seconds.

3. Taste for sweetness, adding agave nectar if desired.

Nutrition per serving: 153 calories; 2g protein; 3g fat (2g sat. fat); 33g carbohydrates;
6g fiber; 20g sugars; 11mg sodium; 88mg calcium; 1mg iron; 582mg potassium; 111mg
Vitamin C; 356IU Vitamin A

PAPAYA PLEASER

Makes 2 smoothies

Confession: On its own, papaya isn't my favorite fruit.
But this ultra-silky smoothie is so scrumptious, I just may become
a papaya fanatic yet.

⅓ CUP COCONUT MILK

⅓ CUP ORANGE JUICE

1¾ CUPS CHOPPED PAPAYA
(ABOUT 1 MEDIUM)

1 BANANA, SLICED AND FROZEN

1 Add all of the ingredients to the
blender, starting with the liquids.

2 Cover and blend until smooth,
about 30 seconds.

Nutrition per serving: 127 calories; 1g protein; 1g fat (1g sat. fat); 30g carbohydrates;
3g fiber; 20g sugars; 12mg sodium; 39mg calcium; 1mg iron; 415mg potassium; 69mg
Vitamin C; 1035IU Vitamin A

CAN'T-MISS CANTALOUPE

Makes 2 smoothies

Pale orange and refreshing, this smoothie isn't super thick,
but it has a lovely fresh cantaloupe taste. Use green grapes for
the prettiest color. To make ice pops, simply pour the smoothie
into molds and freeze for a few hours. Paper cups and
Popsicle sticks will also do the trick.

¼ CUP UNSWEETENED ALMOND MILK

2½ CUPS CUBED CANTALOUPE

½ CUP FROZEN PINEAPPLE CHUNKS

½ CUP FROZEN GRAPES

1. Add all of the ingredients to the blender, starting with the almond milk.

2. Cover and blend until smooth, about 30 seconds.

Nutrition per serving: 109 calories; 2g protein; 1g fat (0g sat. fat); 26g carbohydrates;
3g fiber; 24g sugars; 55mg sodium; 52mg calcium; 1mg iron; 647mg potassium; 94mg
Vitamin C; 6873IU Vitamin A

TROPICAL DELIGHT

Makes 2 smoothies

When I whipped up this smoothie I realized that the taste is
strikingly similar to my mom's homemade "Orange Julius."
Even better, its creamy, smooth texture is to die for. Make sure to use
a ripe mango, and snap up a champagne, or Ataulfo, variety if you
can find one. They are smoother and less fibrous than their more
common Tommy Atkins cousins.

¾ CUP COCONUT MILK

½ CUP ORANGE JUICE

1 CUP CHOPPED MANGO
(ABOUT 1 MEDIUM)

1 CUP FROZEN PINEAPPLE CHUNKS

1 Add all of the ingredients to the blender, starting with the liquids.

2 Cover and blend until smooth, about 30 seconds.

Nutrition per serving: 151 calories; 1g protein; 2g fat (2g sat. fat); 36g carbohydrates;
3g fiber; 28g sugars; 9mg sodium; 59mg calcium; 1mg iron; 288mg potassium; 79mg
Vitamin C; 1155IU Vitamin A

MOM'S MANGO LASSI

Makes 2 smoothies

I make this sweet yet tart smoothie so often it has been dubbed "mine." Lightly spiced and a beautiful pale orange, it's a refreshing take on India's healthy yogurt-based drinks.

1 CUP COCONUT MILK

½ CUP PLAIN GREEK YOGURT

1 CUP CHOPPED MANGO (ABOUT 1 MEDIUM)

¾ CUP FROZEN MANGO CHUNKS

1 TEASPOON HONEY

¼ TEASPOON GROUND CINNAMON

⅛ TEASPOON GROUND CARDAMOM

1 Add all of the ingredients to the blender, starting with the coconut milk.

2 Cover and blend until smooth, about 30 seconds.

Nutrition per serving: 218 calories; 6g protein; 10g fat (4g sat. fat); 31g carbohydrates; 4g fiber; 26g sugars; 60mg sodium; 95mg calcium; 1mg iron; 289mg potassium; 70mg Vitamin C; 3244IU Vitamin A

PINEAPPLE-BASIL

Makes 2 smoothies

When I sip certain smoothies I'm transported to a
beautiful sandy beach. When I sip this smoothie I'm transported
to a beautiful sandy beach… in Thailand, thanks to the basil and
ginger. While it might seem strange to add a savory herb to a
smoothie, basil has a slight licorice note and in small quantities
it adds a beguiling, exotic flavor.

1 CUP COCONUT MILK

1 BANANA

1½ CUPS FROZEN PINEAPPLE CHUNKS

2 BASIL LEAVES, TORN

⅛ TEASPOON PEELED AND GRATED
GINGER, OPTIONAL

1 Add all of the ingredients to
the blender, starting with the
coconut milk.

2 Cover and blend until smooth,
about 30 seconds.

Nutrition per serving: 149 calories; 1g protein; 3g fat (2g sat. fat); 34g carbohydrates;
4g fiber; 23g sugars; 9mg sodium; 69mg calcium; 1mg iron; 391mg potassium; 64mg
Vitamin C; 360IU Vitamin A

BLUEBERRY PANCAKE

Makes 2 smoothies

This pretty purple slurp is a quick and healthy alternative to a stack of blueberry pancakes. It's sweet from the blueberries and syrupy from the, well, syrup. Yogurt stands in for buttermilk, giving the drink a hint of tang. I like the sweet creaminess of regular milk here, but feel free to substitute coconut milk for a tropical twist.

1 CUP MILK

⅔ CUP PLAIN GREEK YOGURT

1¼ CUPS FROZEN BLUEBERRIES

½ TEASPOON VANILLA EXTRACT

⅛ TEASPOON GROUND CINNAMON

2 TABLESPOONS MAPLE SYRUP, PLUS MORE TO TASTE

1. Add all of the ingredients to the blender, starting with the milk.

2. Cover and blend until smooth, about 30 seconds.

3. Taste for sweetness, adding more maple syrup if desired.

Nutrition per serving: 294 calories; 12g protein; 13g fat (5g sat. fat); 36g carbohydrates; 4g fiber; 21g sugars; 142mg sodium; 219mg calcium; 2mg iron; 303mg potassium; 36mg Vitamin C; 2449IU Vitamin A

LYCHEE LOVE

Makes 2 smoothies

Lychees almost taste like perfume—and I mean that in a good way!
They add an enticing fragrant note to this otherwise classic smoothie.

1 CUP COCONUT MILK

1 BANANA

½ CUP CANNED LYCHEES, DRAINED

½ CUP FROZEN PINEAPPLE CHUNKS

½ CUP FROZEN STRAWBERRIES

1 Add all of the ingredients to the blender, starting with the coconut milk.

2 Cover and blend until smooth, about 30 seconds.

Nutrition per serving: 210 calories; 1g protein; 3g fat (2g sat. fat); 50g carbohydrates; 4g fiber; 39g sugars; 19mg sodium; 64mg calcium; 1mg iron; 356mg potassium; 46mg Vitamin C; 316IU Vitamin A

POMEGRANATE-APPLE

Makes 2 smoothies

The apple flavor really shines through in this sweet smoothie. I prefer crunchy eating apples like Gala, Honeycrisp, or Fuji varieties, but for a tarter drink sub in a Granny Smith, or use any other apple you like. Two ingredient notes: There's no need to peel the apple, and red grapes will make for the most appealing color.

½ CUP POMEGRANATE JUICE OR A POMEGRANATE JUICE BLEND

½ CUP UNSWEETENED ALMOND MILK

½ CUP PLAIN GREEK YOGURT

1 APPLE, CORED AND CHOPPED

1½ CUPS FROZEN GRAPES

1 Add all of the ingredients to the blender, starting with the liquids.

2 Cover and blend until smooth, about 30 seconds.

Nutrition per serving: 185 calories; 6g protein; 3g fat (1g sat. fat); 37g carbohydrates; 3g fiber; 32g sugars; 78mg sodium; 160mg calcium; 1mg iron; 407mg potassium; 7mg Vitamin C; 270IU Vitamin A

GINGER-PEAR

Makes 2 smoothies

To my mind, the perfect pear should boast sweet, pale, creamy flesh.
It should be fresh, juicy, and almost tender enough to eat with a
spoon. That said, use canned pears in a pinch. The ginger adds
a subtle zing, but the smoothie is also perfectly delicious without it.

1 CUP UNSWEETENED ALMOND MILK

1 MEDIUM PEAR, CORED AND CUT INTO
CHUNKS (ABOUT 1 CUP)

1 BANANA, SLICED AND FROZEN

⅛ TEASPOON PEELED AND GRATED GINGER

AGAVE NECTAR, OPTIONAL

1. Add the almond milk, pear, banana, and ginger to the blender, starting with the almond milk.

2. Cover and blend until smooth, about 30 seconds.

3. Taste for sweetness, adding agave nectar if desired.

Nutrition per serving: 130 calories; 1g protein; 2g fat (0g sat. fat); 30g carbohydrates;
5g fiber; 19g sugars; 76mg sodium; 160mg calcium; 1mg iron; 399mg potassium; 8.5mg
Vitamin C; 306IU Vitamin A

COCO-DATE

Makes 2 smoothies

When my husband and I were first dating, we went to Morocco
together for a week. (Great way to ease into a relationship, right?)
I will never forget picking dates off trees near the Sahara or drooling
in front of stands piled high with different varieties of dates in
Marrakech. I have had a passion for the sticky fruit ever since, and
I would choose this exotic-tasting smoothie over a more traditional
dessert most days of the week.

1½ CUPS COCONUT MILK

6 DATES, PREFERABLY MEDJOOL, PITTED

2 BANANAS, SLICED AND FROZEN

1 TEASPOON VANILLA EXTRACT

¼ TEASPOON GROUND CINNAMON

⅛ TEASPOON GROUND CARDAMOM

1 Add all of the ingredients to the blender, starting with the coconut milk.

2 Cover and blend until smooth, about 30 seconds.

Nutrition per serving: 358 calories; 3g protein; 4g fat (3g sat. fat); 87g carbohydrates;
9g fiber; 67g sugars; 13mg sodium; 130mg calcium; 2mg iron; 992mg potassium; 10mg
Vitamin C; 559IU Vitamin A

APRICOT-CHERRY JAM

Teaming up apricots and cherries makes for a
sweet smoothie with a flavor that really pops. The almond extract
adds a bit of nutty intensity.

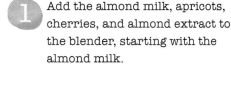

1 CUP UNSWEETENED ALMOND MILK

4 RIPE APRICOTS, PITTED

1 CUP FROZEN CHERRIES

⅛ TEASPOON ALMOND EXTRACT

MAPLE SYRUP, OPTIONAL

1. Add the almond milk, apricots, cherries, and almond extract to the blender, starting with the almond milk.

2. Cover and blend until smooth, about 30 seconds.

3. Taste for sweetness, adding maple syrup if desired.

Nutrition per serving: 102 calories; 2g protein; 2g fat (0g sat. fat); 21g carbohydrates; 4g fiber; 16g sugars; 90mg sodium; 119mg calcium; 1mg iron; 447mg potassium; 12mg Vitamin C; 1647IU Vitamin A

VEG-TASTIC

2

For X-Ray Vision

Ruby Red and Delicious

Smoothie Supercharger

Ultra Creamy

VEGETABLES ARE WHAT MAKE

smoothies so cool. Add a handful of spinach or a bit of beet and you have a super-charged drink that is still delicious. Leafy greens are a popular pick because they virtually disappear into a drink. Avocados are like smoothie superheroes, adding a luscious creaminess to any drink they grace with their presence. Beets, carrots, and sweet potatoes are also stellar smoothie players. Their natural sweetness and nutrient content simply push the drinks' health quotient higher and higher. Here is a rundown on the star qualities of my favorite veggies.

Avocado If I had to nominate an MVV (Most Valuable Vegetable) in the smoothie category, I would choose an avocado, no question. (Let's agree not to quibble about the fact that avocados are technically fruits.) Aside from giving smoothies an almost luxurious creaminess, avocados are also bursting with vitamins and minerals, including copper, folate, potassium, Vitamin K, and Vitamin E. Yes, avocados' velvety texture comes thanks to the high fat content, but don't let that scare you. The avocado's fats are incredibly beneficial. They contain anti-inflammatory properties, contribute to heart health, and aid in the absorption of fat-soluble Vitamins A, E, D, and K. Healthy and delicious? Avocados have my vote: MVV all the way.

Spinach My favorite way to incorporate this calcium- and fiber-rich green is to have a container of pre-washed baby spinach on hand. While washing a bunch of spinach may be less expensive, the convenience of pre-washed can't be beat, and the flavor of baby spinach is much milder. Spinach is full of good things like Vitamins A and K, manganese, and folate. One note: Conventionally grown spinach can be high in pesticides, so consider buying organic. For most of the smoothies in this book, baby kale and baby spinach are interchangeable.

Kale I recently joked that it was against the law to have a dinner party in Brooklyn without serving kale (although maybe you'd get a pass if Brussels sprouts were on the table), and I suspect that it's also illegal to publish a new cookbook without this trendy super green somewhere in residence. Happily, kale is popular for a reason. It's tough to find a vegetable that's as full of Vitamin K, Vitamin C, lutein (for eye health), and calcium (for strong teeth and bones). There are numerous varieties of kale. For smoothies my favorites are either pre-washed and packaged baby kale or a bunch of tender lacinato kale. (Traditional curly kale will work as well, but it has a stronger, more bitter flavor.) If I buy lacinato, also called Tuscan kale, I make a habit of washing and prepping it as soon as I get home or at least well before I intend to use it. First, cut out and discard the thick ribs in the center of each leaf. Then wash the kale well and dry it; I use a salad spinner. Place the cleaned kale in a zip-top plastic bag with a paper towel and refrigerate for up to five days. The kale will stay fresh and you'll always have some green available for your smoothies.

Beets Beets are unbeatable in smoothies. Aside from their enviable nutritional stats—full of folate and manganese, among other minerals—they boast a natural sweetness and a drop-dead awesome color. Like adults, kids eat first with their eyes, so a bright red smoothie can be instantly enticing. While beets are sweet they also have an earthy quality that turns some people off. To temper that, simply combine them with strongly flavored fruits like cherries and raspberries, or add a bit of sweetener. Once again I go for convenience when buying beets. I like the precooked and vacuum-packed beets in the produce section of my grocery store. (Melissa's and LOVE are two popular brands.) Of course, feel free to steam or roast raw beets yourself. Beets will add serious nutrition to your shakes any way they're prepped.

Sweet Potatoes and Pumpkin

In addition to contributing a boatload of beta-carotene, sweet potatoes and pumpkin add sweetness and silkiness to these drinks. When using pumpkin, canned is the way to go; just make sure to pick pure pumpkin, not pumpkin pie filling. Canned sweet potatoes are also convenient, although I love the vegetable's caramelized flavor when roasted. Simply wash the sweet potatoes and bake in a 425°F oven until tender, usually 35 to 45 minutes depending on the vegetable's size. Spoon the flesh from the skin and use when cooled or refrigerate for up to five days.

Carrots While I don't use carrots often in smoothies, they shouldn't be overlooked. When steamed until soft, they blend easily and lend an appealing bright color to drinks. Like their orange cousins above, carrots are full of beta-carotene, which is converted into Vitamin A in the body. Carrots are also a good source of potassium, Vitamin K, and Vitamin C.

AVOCADO BLISS

Makes 2 smoothies

This lovely, creamy green smoothie isn't overly sweet, so its mild coconut flavor really shines through. The kids might appreciate a dollop of agave blended in.

2 CUPS COCONUT MILK

1 RIPE AVOCADO, CUT INTO CHUNKS

1 CUP BABY SPINACH

1 CUP FROZEN MANGO CHUNKS

AGAVE NECTAR, OPTIONAL

1. Add the coconut milk, avocado, spinach, and mango to the blender, starting with the coconut milk.

2. Cover and blend until smooth, about 30 seconds.

3. Taste for sweetness, adding agave nectar if desired.

Nutrition per serving: 240 calories; 3g protein; 15g fat (6g sat. fat); 27g carbohydrates; 8g fiber; 19g sugars; 43mg sodium; 145mg calcium; 2mg iron; 573mg potassium; 44mg Vitamin C; 3326IU Vitamin A

CHOCOLATE-BANANA GREEN MACHINE

Makes 2 smoothies

"You're the best mom in the world." That's what my daughter said when I gave her this smoothie one morning. Who could blame her? Thick, creamy, and chocolaty, it was like I offered her a milkshake for breakfast. The one thing this smoothie isn't is spinach-y. For a dairy-free vegan version, substitute chocolate soymilk.

1½ CUPS CHOCOLATE MILK

1 TABLESPOON UNSWEETENED COCOA POWDER

1½ CUPS BABY SPINACH

1½ BANANAS, SLICED AND FROZEN

1. Add all of the ingredients to the blender, starting with the chocolate milk.

2. Cover and blend until smooth, about 30 seconds.

Nutrition per serving: 250 calories; 8g protein; 7g fat (4g sat. fat); 43g carbohydrates; 6g fiber; 29g sugars; 146mg sodium; 258mg calcium; 2mg iron; 671mg potassium; 21mg Vitamin C; 2990IU Vitamin A

KIWI-KALE KOOLER

Makes 2 smoothies

This pretty green drink is another opportunity to showcase avocado's lush creaminess. Unsweetened, the flavor is a touch vegetal, but if you're feeding family members with a sweet tooth, a touch of agave will do the trick.

1½ CUPS UNSWEETENED ALMOND MILK

2 KIWIS, PEELED AND CHOPPED INTO CHUNKS

2 CUPS CHOPPED KALE

½ RIPE AVOCADO, CUT INTO CHUNKS

½ CUP FROZEN GRAPES

AGAVE NECTAR, OPTIONAL

1. Add the almond milk, kiwis, kale, avocado, and grapes to the blender, starting with the almond milk.

2. Cover and blend until smooth, about 30 seconds.

3. Taste for sweetness, adding agave nectar if desired.

Nutrition per serving: 178 calories; 5g protein; 8g fat (1g sat. fat); 25g carbohydrates; 7g fiber; 10g sugars; 168mg sodium; 272mg calcium; 2mg iron; 874mg potassium; 148mg Vitamin C; 10,810IU Vitamin A

COCONUT-CARROT

Makes 2 smoothies

This brilliant orange-colored smoothie tastes of apple, mango, and coconut. The lemon juice intensifies the flavors, but it does make the smoothie a bit more tart, so follow your taste buds.

1½ CUPS COCONUT MILK

¾ CUP CHOPPED STEAMED CARROTS, CHILLED

1 SMALL APPLE, CORED AND CHOPPED

¾ CUP FROZEN MANGO CHUNKS

2 TEASPOONS LEMON JUICE, OPTIONAL

1. Add all of the ingredients to the blender, starting with the coconut milk.

2. Cover and blend until smooth, about 30 seconds.

3. Taste and add the lemon juice if desired.

Nutrition per serving: 148 calories; 1g protein; 4g fat (3g sat. fat); 30g carbohydrates; 5g fiber; 24g sugars; 46mg sodium; 102mg calcium; 1mg iron; 405mg potassium; 29mg Vitamin C; 9105IU Vitamin A

PEACHY KEEN

Makes 2 smoothies

While I am usually a fan of frozen fruit, seek out a fresh, ripe, juicy peach for this lovely, almond-y smoothie. The taste is incomparable.

1 CUP MILK

1½ CUPS CHOPPED FRESH PEACHES
(SKIN ON IS FINE)

1 CUP BABY SPINACH

1 CUP FROZEN BLACKBERRIES

⅛ TEASPOON ALMOND EXTRACT

1 TEASPOON AGAVE NECTAR,
PLUS MORE TO TASTE

1. Add all of the ingredients to the blender, starting with the milk.

2. Cover and blend until smooth, about 30 seconds.

3. Taste for sweetness, adding more agave nectar if desired.

Nutrition per serving: 151 calories; 7g protein; 3g fat (2g sat. fat); 27g carbohydrates; 6g fiber; 16g sugars; 74mg sodium; 193mg calcium; 1mg iron; 611mg potassium; 28mg Vitamin C; 2190IU Vitamin A

DON'T SAY POTATO

Makes 2 smoothies

While I'm not usually one for sneaking veggies, it pays to know your audience. If you have choosy eaters on your hands, feel free to call this a pineapple-orange smoothie. No one will ever know there is sweet potato in this beautiful, brilliant orange drink. They'll taste the bright pineapple and orange flavors, and you'll be happy they're getting a good dose of fiber and Vitamin C, plus tons of Vitamin A.

¾ CUP ORANGE JUICE

½ CUP COCONUT MILK

1 CUP MASHED, COOKED SWEET POTATO

1 CUP FROZEN PINEAPPLE CHUNKS

¼ TEASPOON GROUND CINNAMON

1 TEASPOON HONEY, PLUS MORE TO TASTE

1. Add all of the ingredients to the blender, starting with the liquids.

2. Cover and blend until smooth, about 30 seconds.

3. Taste for sweetness, adding more honey if desired.

Nutrition per serving: 248 calories; 3g protein; 2g fat (1g sat. fat); 58g carbohydrates; 4g fiber; 28g sugars; 102mg sodium; 76mg calcium; 2mg iron; 421mg potassium; 60mg Vitamin C; 11,305IU Vitamin A

MEGA GREEN

Makes 2 smoothies

I went back and forth on the name for this smoothie. Mega Green? It is indeed. Salad-in-a-Glass? That would also fit. Whatever you call it, this ultra-healthy green sip feels virtuous and tastes fresh and revitalizing. If the smoothie is too thick for your taste, thin it out with a bit more coconut milk. There's no need to peel the cucumber.

1¼ CUPS COCONUT MILK

½ CUP BABY KALE OR BABY SPINACH

½ RIPE AVOCADO, CUT INTO CHUNKS

¾ CUP CUCUMBER CHUNKS

1 CUP FROZEN GREEN GRAPES

¼ TEASPOON PEELED AND GRATED GINGER

AGAVE NECTAR, TO TASTE

1. Add all of the ingredients to the blender, starting with the coconut milk.

2. Cover and blend until smooth, about 30 seconds.

3. Taste for sweetness, adding agave nectar if desired.

Nutrition per serving: 163 calories; 2g protein; 10g fat (4g sat. fat); 19g carbohydrates; 5g fiber; 13g sugars; 25mg sodium; 93mg calcium; 2mg iron; 429mg potassium; 12mg Vitamin C; 1376IU Vitamin A

ROCKET FUEL

Makes 2 smoothies

As I was developing recipes for this book, I asked my daughter what smoothie she'd like to create. She quickly answered, "Rocket fuel." Okay then! Well, rocket fuel should certainly be super-healthy, high-octane in fact, full of nutritious fruits and even vegetables for extra power. But, even more than that, I wanted it to be red. This smoothie is certainly that—a gorgeous, bright purple-red. It's also a bit sweet, a bit sour, and a lot tasty, either as a smoothie or frozen into ice pops.

¾ CUP POMEGRANATE JUICE

¼ CUP WATER

½ CUP CHOPPED COOKED BEETS
(ABOUT 1 MEDIUM)

1 CUP FROZEN RASPBERRIES

1 CUP FROZEN CHERRIES

1. Add all of the ingredients to the blender, starting with the liquids.

2. Cover and blend until smooth, about 30 seconds.

Nutrition per serving: 150 calories; 2g protein; 1g fat (0g sat. fat); 36g carbohydrates; 7g fiber; 28g sugars; 43mg sodium; 43mg calcium; 1mg iron; 594mg potassium; 23mg Vitamin C; 84IU Vitamin A

NO FOOLIN' APPLE-BEET

Makes 2 smoothies

Sometimes when I'm on a health kick, I'll buy a pressed juice at a popular spot in my neighborhood. It runs me about $8 (eek!), but tastes fresh and healthy and gingery. I don't visit juice bars very often because of the price, of course, but also because I want the fiber that comes from blending whole fruits and vegetables. This smoothie is my take on that vibrant juice. There's no mistaking the beets here, and that's just how I like it.

1 CUP UNSWEETENED ALMOND MILK

2 MEDIUM COOKED BEETS, CHOPPED

1 APPLE, CORED AND CHOPPED

1 CUP FROZEN GRAPES

⅛ TEASPOON PEELED AND GRATED GINGER

1 TEASPOON LEMON JUICE

1. Add all of the ingredients to the blender, starting with the almond milk.

2. Cover and blend until smooth, about 30 seconds.

Nutrition per serving: 119 calories; 2g protein; 2g fat (0g sat. fat); 26g carbohydrates; 5g fiber; 20g sugars; 156mg sodium; 124mg calcium; 1mg iron; 519mg potassium; 10mg Vitamin C; 358IU Vitamin A

PUMPKIN PIE SMOOTHIE

Makes 2 smoothies

My idea of heaven is leftover pie for breakfast; it's a good thing I rarely have partially eaten pies lying around. Imagine my delight when I whipped up this pumpkin pie smoothie. It's rich, creamy, and craveable, yet packed with Vitamin A and fiber, making it totally appropriate for breakfast. Voilà! I'm able to have my pie and eat it too.

1½ CUPS COCONUT MILK

1 CUP CANNED PUMPKIN

2 DATES, PREFERABLY MEDJOOL, PITTED

1 BANANA, SLICED AND FROZEN

¾ TEASPOON VANILLA EXTRACT

¾ TEASPOON GROUND CINNAMON

¾ TEASPOON GROUND CLOVES

⅛ TEASPOON GROUND NUTMEG

1 TABLESPOON MAPLE SYRUP, PLUS MORE TO TASTE

1. Add all of the ingredients to the blender, starting with the coconut milk.

2. Cover and blend until smooth, about 30 seconds.

3. Taste for sweetness, adding more maple syrup if desired.

Nutrition per serving: 244 calories; 3g protein; 4g fat (3g sat. fat); 55g carbohydrates; 8g fiber; 39g sugars; 21mg sodium; 150mg calcium; 3mg iron; 732mg potassium; 11mg Vitamin C; 1952IU Vitamin A

POWER UP

3

Chia Seeds

Acai

1/4 TSP

1/2 TSP - 2.5 ml

1 TSP - 5 ml

1 TBSP - 15 ml

Tofu

Almond
Butter

Greek
Yogurt

Oats

Ground Flaxseeds

1 Table Spoon
15.0 cc

EVEN FRUIT- AND VEGGIE-PACKED SMOOTHIES CAN USE

a boost. Each of the smoothies in this chapter boasts one or more superfoods that will add even more powerful nutrition to your or your child's day. Here's the scoop: While these superfoods are found primarily in this chapter, feel free to add a tablespoon or two of ground flax or hemp seeds to any of the smoothies in this book. The texture may change slightly, but the smoothie's nutritional power will only be enhanced.

Nuts and Nut Butters Almonds, peanuts, cashews, walnuts, and macadamias... nuts add body to smoothies and are just downright delicious. But they are also amazingly nutritious. In addition to individual vitamins and minerals, nuts are full of protein, healthy fats, and fiber that help keep us full longer. When choosing a nut butter, look for salt-free, unsweetened varieties (sadly, Nutella doesn't count here). It's also easy to make your own. Just blend your nut of choice in the food processor with a little canola oil until smooth. If there are nut allergies in your household, sunflower butter is a good swap for peanut or almond butter in any of these recipes.

Chia Seeds If you still think of fluffy "pets" when chia seeds come to mind, it's time to think again. Tiny chia seeds contain a lot of nutrition in a small package, including high amounts of omega-3 fatty acids, fiber, phosphorous, and magnesium. They are also a complete protein. While chia seeds may be a relatively new food to us, their nutritional benefits are not a recent discovery. The Aztecs called chia seeds the "running food" since just a few spoonfuls could keep a literally on-the-run messenger satiated and powered during an arduous mission. Chia seeds also perform a bit of culinary magic. Soak them in liquid for 10 minutes or more and they start to swell, thickening the liquid and giving it an almost gelatin-like quality.

Silken Tofu Tofu may be a vegetarian's delight, but it is also a smoothie-maker's friend. Soft and jiggly, silken tofu gives body and creaminess to smoothies, plus a boost of protein. Make sure to purchase silken tofu and not firm or extra-firm.

Ground Flaxseeds Flaxseeds have a glowing nutritional reputation and for good reason. They are high in fiber, a good source of plant omega-3 fatty acids, and a source of beneficial phytochemicals called lignans. They are also mild in flavor and play well with a multitude of other foods. Flaxseeds give smoothies a thicker texture and a bit of "chew." Our bodies can't absorb whole flaxseeds, so buy them already ground and store them in the refrigerator for maximum freshness.

Hemp Seeds Hemp seeds may sound illicit, but they are actually a perfectly safe (and legal!) source of essential fatty acids, potassium, and iron. Like quinoa and chia seeds, they are also one of the few plant-based sources of complete protein. Hemp seeds are ideal smoothie partners. Since they are relatively soft, they blend up nicely, and their mild taste is never distracting.

Oats Good old-fashioned oats are high in protein and fiber, and they add a nutty, full-bodied quality to smoothies. While you can add a handful of raw oats to smoothies, I prefer adding cooked oatmeal. Simply prepare a small quantity of unsweetened instant oats in the microwave, let cool for a few minutes, and blend.

Acai Antioxidant-rich acai is a tart-tasting, dark purple berry native to the South American rainforest. To make life easier I buy it already pureed and frozen into convenient smoothie packs. Look for brands like Sambazon. Be sure to buy the unsweetened variety, and pair it with fresh fruits for a naturally sweet taste.

Greek Yogurt This universally popular dairy product appears in other chapters in this book, but it truly does power up already healthy smoothies. When I first tasted Greek yogurt several years back, I could hardly believe my taste buds. Could something this creamy really be good for me? Luckily, protein and calcium-rich Greek yogurt is not too good to be true, with one big caveat: Buy the plain version. Like most flavored yogurts, sweetened Greek yogurt, even vanilla, often has three or more teaspoons of added sugar per serving. In general, I skip fat-free dairy, since some fat is necessary for nutrient absorption and to help us feel full. I prefer creamy 2 percent Greek yogurt in my smoothies (just as I drink 2 percent milk). Remember, though, that children under age two should consume full-fat dairy.

BLUEBERRY-ALMOND BASH

Makes 2 smoothies

Simple and delicious, this smoothie is as wholesome as it gets. I love it
for breakfast, but it's also a stellar afternoon snack.

1½ CUPS UNSWEETENED ALMOND MILK

2 BANANAS

1 CUP FROZEN BLUEBERRIES

2 TABLESPOONS ALMOND BUTTER

MAPLE SYRUP, OPTIONAL

1. Add the almond milk, bananas, blueberries, and almond butter to the blender, starting with the almond milk.

2. Cover and blend until smooth, about 30 seconds.

3. Taste for sweetness, adding maple syrup if desired.

Nutrition per serving: 275 calories; 6g protein; 12g fat (1g sat. fat); 42g
carbohydrates; 7g fiber; 22g sugars; 138mg sodium; 216mg calcium; 1mg iron; 740mg
potassium; 17mg Vitamin C; 490IU Vitamin A

SUPERFOOD SMOOTHIE
(AKA HEMP TO CHOCOLATE-BANANA)

Makes 2 smoothies

Combined with antioxidant-rich cherries, cocoa powder, and acai,
this hemp-rich smoothie is exceptionally nutritious. Happily, it is also
exceptionally scrumptious.

1½ CUPS UNSWEETENED ALMOND MILK

1½ BANANAS

3 TABLESPOONS HEMP SEEDS

ONE 3.5-OZ. PACKAGE FROZEN
UNSWEETENED ACAI

½ CUP FROZEN CHERRIES

1 TABLESPOON UNSWEETENED
COCOA POWDER

1½ TEASPOONS MAPLE SYRUP,
PLUS MORE TO TASTE

1. Add all of the ingredients to the blender, starting with the almond milk.

2. Cover and blend until smooth, about 30 seconds.

3. Taste for sweetness, adding more maple syrup if desired.

Nutrition per serving: 300 calories; 9g protein; 13g fat (2g sat. fat); 43g carbohydrates; 6g fiber; 26g sugars; 143mg sodium; 188mg calcium; 2mg iron; 618mg potassium; 10mg Vitamin C; 831IU Vitamin A

GRAPE NUTS

Makes 2 smoothies

This sweet smoothie packs a double punch of nuts. You can find cashew butter at many large grocery stores or natural food markets, or it's easy enough to make your own by grinding cashews in a food processor with a pinch of salt. Of course, feel free to sub in almond butter or peanut butter.

1 CUP UNSWEETENED ALMOND MILK

1 CUP CHOPPED APPLE (ABOUT 1 MEDIUM)

1 CUP FROZEN GRAPES

3 TABLESPOONS CASHEW BUTTER

HONEY, OPTIONAL

1 Add the almond milk, apple, grapes, and cashew butter to the blender, starting with the almond milk.

2 Cover and blend until smooth, about 30 seconds.

3 Taste for sweetness, adding honey if desired.

Nutrition per serving: 224 calories; 5g protein; 14g fat (3g sat. fat); 24g carbohydrates; 3g fiber; 14g sugars; 95mg sodium; 121mg calcium; 1mg iron; 381mg potassium; 5mg Vitamin C; 331IU Vitamin A

HAWAIIAN BREEZE

Makes 2 smoothies

Wow, I could drink this all day! Fiber-filled macadamia nuts add a buttery richness that takes this smoothie over the top.

1¼ CUPS COCONUT MILK

1 CUP CHOPPED PAPAYA (ABOUT 1 MEDIUM)

¾ CUP FROZEN PINEAPPLE CHUNKS

¾ CUP FROZEN MANGO CHUNKS

¼ CUP UNSALTED MACADAMIA NUTS

1. Add all of the ingredients to the blender, starting with the coconut milk.

2. Cover and blend until smooth, about 30 seconds.

Nutrition per serving: 263 calories; 3g protein; 16g fat (5g sat. fat); 33g carbohydrates; 5g fiber; 25g sugars; 17mg sodium; 106mg calcium; 2mg iron; 421mg potassium; 96mg Vitamin C; 1707IU Vitamin A

CHIA-POMEGRANATE CHILLER

Makes 2 smoothies

If chia's remarkable nutritional powers aren't enough to convince you to try this drink, consider the alluring combination of sweet and tart pomegranate and exotic vanilla. You won't be disappointed.

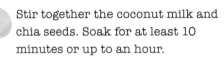

1 CUP COCONUT MILK

2 TABLESPOONS CHIA SEEDS

1 BANANA, SLICED AND FROZEN

1 CUP POMEGRANATE JUICE

½ TEASPOON VANILLA EXTRACT

AGAVE NECTAR, OPTIONAL

1. Stir together the coconut milk and chia seeds. Soak for at least 10 minutes or up to an hour.

2. Add the chia seeds and coconut milk to the blender, along with the banana, pomegranate juice, and vanilla.

3. Cover and blend until smooth, about 30 seconds.

4. Taste for sweetness, adding agave nectar if desired.

Nutrition per serving: 224 calories; 3g protein; 7g fat (3g sat. fat); 40g carbohydrates; 8g fiber; 27g sugars; 22mg sodium; 156mg calcium; 2mg iron; 545mg potassium; 6mg Vitamin C; 295IU Vitamin A

PB & J

Makes 2 smoothies

I am a peanut butter addict. From peanut butter cookies to peanut butter sandwiches to peanut butter on a spoon, if there's peanut butter, count me in. Naturally a PB & J smoothie had to be concocted, and, I have to say, this one really tastes like the classic sandwich. Use any frozen grapes you have on hand, but this is especially pretty with red ones. After a few tries with raw oats I discovered that using cooked oatmeal adds an appealing "bready" taste. Simply microwave ¼ cup instant oats with ½ cup water for 1 minute, and you're good to go.

1 CUP UNSWEETENED ALMOND MILK

1 BANANA

1 CUP FROZEN GRAPES

2 TABLESPOONS CREAMY PEANUT BUTTER

½ CUP COOKED OATMEAL, COOLED

1. Add all of the ingredients to the blender, starting with the almond milk.

2. Cover and blend until smooth, about 30 seconds.

Nutrition per serving: 235 calories; 7g protein; 10g fat (2g sat. fat); 32g carbohydrates; 5g fiber; 16g sugars; 138mg sodium; 125mg calcium; 1mg iron; 435mg potassium; 7mg Vitamin C; 334IU Vitamin A

HONEY-PEACH

Makes 2 smoothies

There is nothing like a ripe summer peach. Fragrant, sweet, and dripping with juice, in season peaches are truly one of life's most delicious pleasures. Thankfully, frozen peaches can ably fill the gap the other 10 months of the year. Blended with ground flaxseeds—a superfood high in fiber and plant omega-3 fatty acids—peaches and honey make for a mild, cream-colored drink with a bit of texture. Don't skip the lemon; it really brings out the flavor of the peaches.

1 CUP MILK

⅔ CUP PLAIN GREEK YOGURT

1⅓ CUPS FROZEN PEACH SLICES

¼ CUP GROUND FLAXSEEDS

1 TEASPOON LEMON JUICE

2 TABLESPOONS HONEY

1 Add all of the ingredients to the blender, starting with the milk.

2 Cover and blend until smooth, about 30 seconds.

Nutrition per serving: 377 calories; 15g protein; 19g fat (6g sat. fat); 41g carbohydrates; 7g fiber; 26g sugars; 156mg sodium; 265mg calcium; 2mg iron; 544mg potassium; 35mg Vitamin C; 2727IU Vitamin A

BERRY-ACAI ICE

Makes 2 smoothies

Combined with fresh blackberries—or blueberries if you prefer—
the acai makes for a gorgeous, dark purple drink.

1 CUP COCONUT MILK	 **1** Add all of the ingredients to the blender, starting with the coconut milk.
1 BANANA	
1 CUP BLACKBERRIES	**2** Cover and blend until smooth, about 30 seconds.
1 CUP FROZEN MIXED BERRIES	
ONE 3.5-OZ. PACKAGE FROZEN UNSWEETENED ACAI	**3** Taste for sweetness, adding more agave nectar if desired.
2 TEASPOONS AGAVE NECTAR, PLUS MORE TO TASTE	

Nutrition per serving: 198 calories; 3g protein; 6g fat (3g sat. fat); 38g carbohydrates;
8g fiber; 24g sugars; 15mg sodium; 96mg calcium; 1mg iron; 489mg potassium; 65mg
Vitamin C; 826IU Vitamin A

GRANOLA BAR IN A GLASS

Makes 2 smoothies

I have a weakness for granola. Sprinkled over yogurt,
baked into bars, or just eaten by the handful out of the bag, a good
granola is irresistible. I wanted to translate that sweet, nutty
goodness into a drink, and this substantial, almond-flavored smoothie
is the tasty result.

1 CUP UNSWEETENED ALMOND MILK

2 DATES, PREFERABLY MEDJOOL, PITTED

1½ CUPS FROZEN GRAPES

½ CUP COOKED OATMEAL, COOLED

2 TABLESPOONS UNSWEETENED
ALMOND BUTTER

2 TABLESPOONS GROUND FLAXSEEDS

1 Add all of the ingredients to the blender, starting with the almond milk.

2 Cover and blend until smooth, about 30 seconds.

Nutrition per serving: 310 calories; 8g protein; 15g fat (1g sat. fat); 43g
carbohydrates; 7g fiber; 28g sugars; 136mg sodium; 204mg calcium; 2mg iron; 611mg
potassium; 3mg Vitamin C; 355IU Vitamin A

PEANUT-BERRY BLAST

Makes 2 smoothies

To my taste, you can't go wrong with peanut butter.
Use any frozen berries you have on hand.

1 CUP UNSWEETENED ALMOND MILK

1 BANANA

1½ CUPS FROZEN MIXED BERRIES

2 TABLESPOONS CREAMY PEANUT BUTTER

½ CUP PLAIN GREEK YOGURT

2 TABLESPOONS GROUND FLAXSEEDS

AGAVE NECTAR, OPTIONAL

1. Add the almond milk, banana, berries, peanut butter, yogurt, and flaxseeds to the blender, starting with the almond milk.

2. Cover and blend until smooth, about 30 seconds.

3. Taste for sweetness, adding agave nectar if desired.

Nutrition per serving: 352 calories; 11g protein; 20g fat (4g sat. fat); 38g carbohydrates; 8g fiber; 18g sugars; 220mg sodium; 156mg calcium; 2mg iron; 447mg potassium; 33mg Vitamin C; 1778IU Vitamin A

I DREAM OF TANGERINE

Makes 2 smoothies

Like avocados and bananas, silken tofu gives smoothies a velvety creaminess. It blends up like a dream in this sunset-colored drink and is virtually flavorless. I prefer tangerines for their bright zing and easy-to-peel exteriors, but oranges are another option.

½ CUP ORANGE JUICE

½ CUP COCONUT MILK

2 SMALL TANGERINES, PEELED AND SEPARATED INTO SEGMENTS (ABOUT 1 CUP), SEEDS REMOVED

1¼ CUPS FROZEN MANGO CHUNKS

½ CUP SILKEN TOFU

AGAVE NECTAR, OPTIONAL

1 Add the orange juice, coconut milk, tangerines, mango, and tofu to the blender, starting with the liquids.

2 Cover and blend until smooth, about 30 seconds.

3 Taste for sweetness, adding agave nectar if desired.

Nutrition per serving: 196 calories; 5g protein; 3g fat (1g sat. fat); 41g carbohydrates; 4g fiber; 33g sugars; 11mg sodium; 91mg calcium; 1mg iron; 486mg potassium; 73mg Vitamin C; 1932IU Vitamin A

APPLE-WALNUT SPINACH

Makes 2 smoothies

Whether it's in salads or smoothies, apples and walnuts play well together. For a creamier consistency, soak the walnuts in water for up to 12 hours ahead of time. Drain and then add to the blender with fresh water. If you forget to soak, no worries. Blend away; the smoothie will just have a bit more texture.

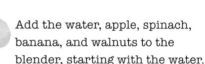

1 CUP COLD WATER

1 APPLE, CORED AND CHOPPED

1 CUP BABY SPINACH

1 BANANA, SLICED AND FROZEN

½ CUP WALNUTS (SOAKED FOR UP TO 12 HOURS)

HONEY, OPTIONAL

1. Add the water, apple, spinach, banana, and walnuts to the blender, starting with the water.

2. Cover and blend until smooth, about 30 seconds.

3. Taste for sweetness, adding honey if desired.

Nutrition per serving: 298 calories; 6g protein; 20g fat (2g sat. fat); 31g carbohydrates; 6g fiber; 17g sugars; 24mg sodium; 64mg calcium; 2mg iron; 438mg potassium; 18mg Vitamin C; 1928IU Vitamin A

FIGS, GRAPES, AND DATES

Makes 2 smoothies

Dried figs and dates are two of my favorite fruits. They are rich, complex, very sweet and, call to mind alfresco meals and exotic locales. This smoothie spotlights these two sumptuous ingredients. The yogurt and cocoa take the edge off their sweetness, and the almond butter adds a punch of protein and Vitamin E. If your dates or figs are more dry than moist, soak them in warm water for 10 minutes before draining and blending.

1¼ CUPS UNSWEETENED ALMOND MILK

2 DRIED MISSION FIGS, CHOPPED

3 DATES, PREFERABLY MEDJOOL, PITTED

1 CUP FROZEN GRAPES

½ CUP PLAIN GREEK YOGURT

2 TABLESPOONS ALMOND BUTTER

3 TEASPOONS UNSWEETENED COCOA POWDER

1. Add all of the ingredients to the blender, starting with the almond milk.

2. Cover and blend until smooth, about 30 seconds.

Nutrition per serving: 367 calories; 10g protein; 19g fat (3g sat. fat); 48g carbohydrates; 8g fiber; 36g sugars; 168mg sodium; 256mg calcium; 2mg iron; 675mg potassium; 19mg Vitamin C; 1845IU Vitamin A

(NOT) BERRY GREEN

Makes 2 smoothies

This smoothie has it all—antioxidant-rich fruit, protein-packed almond butter, and, yes, even spinach. But as the recipe name suggests, this concoction isn't your typical "green smoothie." Let your little veggie-phobes know they're drinking their greens… if you want. Otherwise they will happily sip away at this deep violet drink, none the wiser and all the healthier.

1½ CUPS UNSWEETENED ALMOND MILK

1 BANANA

1 CUP BABY SPINACH

1 CUP FROZEN MIXED BERRIES

2 TABLESPOONS ALMOND BUTTER

1 TABLESPOON AGAVE NECTAR, PLUS MORE TO TASTE

1. Add all of the ingredients to the blender, starting with the almond milk.

2. Cover and blend until smooth, about 30 seconds.

3. Taste for sweetness, adding more agave nectar if desired.

Nutrition per serving: 259 calories; 6g protein; 12g fat (1g sat. fat); 42g carbohydrates; 6g fiber; 27g sugars; 159mg sodium; 239mg calcium; 2mg iron; 529mg potassium; 20mg Vitamin C; 2285IU Vitamin A

BEETS-ME

Makes 2 smoothies

The dusty rose color hints at this smoothie's ingredients, but you'll
be hard-pressed to identify the beets in this creamy, peanutty drink.
Look for pre-cooked and vacuum-packed beets in the produce section.

1½ CUPS UNSWEETENED ALMOND MILK

1 CUP CHOPPED COOKED BEETS
(ABOUT 2 MEDIUM)

1 BANANA, SLICED AND FROZEN

¼ CUP PEANUT BUTTER

1½ TEASPOONS AGAVE NECTAR,
PLUS MORE TO TASTE

1. Add all of the ingredients to the blender, starting with the almond milk.

2. Cover and blend until smooth, about 30 seconds.

3. Taste for sweetness, adding more agave nectar if desired.

Nutrition per serving: 340 calories; 10g protein; 18g fat (3g sat. fat); 40g
carbohydrates; 6g fiber; 25g sugars; 332mg sodium; 259mg calcium; 2mg iron; 796mg
potassium; 8mg Vitamin C; 442IU Vitamin A

KITCHEN SINK SMOOTHIE

Makes 2 smoothies

A few years ago my husband, daughter, and I used to be semi-regulars at a lovely little Italian restaurant. The food was rustic in the best possible way, and that homey quality extended to dessert. *Brutti ma buoni* cookies were always on offer; the name literally translates as "ugly but good." That goes for this smoothie as well. It may not win any beauty pageants, but the sweet, creamy taste more than makes up for its modest looks.

1 CUP UNSWEETENED ALMOND MILK

2 DATES, PREFERABLY MEDJOOL, PITTED

1 CUP BABY SPINACH

1 BANANA

1 BANANA, SLICED AND FROZEN

2 TABLESPOONS ALMOND BUTTER

ONE 3.5-OZ. PACKAGE FROZEN UNSWEETENED ACAI

2 TABLESPOONS GROUND FLAXSEEDS

1. Add all of the ingredients to the blender, starting with the almond milk.

2. Cover and blend until smooth, about 30 seconds.

Nutrition per serving: 369 calories; 8g protein; 16g fat (2g sat. fat); 54g carbohydrates; 10g fiber; 32g sugars; 121mg sodium; 231mg calcium; 2mg iron; 861mg potassium; 18mg Vitamin C; 2570IU Vitamin A

RASPBERRY-MANGO CHIA

Makes 2 smoothies

This sweet smoothie makes for a filling snack thanks to chia's staying power. Combined with a hit of Vitamin C from the mango and more fiber from the raspberries, it's a nutritional trifecta.

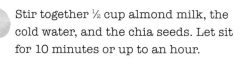

1½ CUPS ALMOND MILK, DIVIDED

¼ CUP COLD WATER

2 TABLESPOONS CHIA SEEDS

1½ CUPS FROZEN MANGO CHUNKS

1 CUP FROZEN RASPBERRIES

AGAVE NECTAR, TO TASTE

1. Stir together ½ cup almond milk, the cold water, and the chia seeds. Let sit for 10 minutes or up to an hour.

2. Add the chia seed mixture to the blender, along with the remaining cup of almond milk, the mango, and the raspberries.

3. Cover and blend until smooth, about 30 seconds.

4. Taste for sweetness, adding agave nectar if desired.

Nutrition per serving: 206 calories; 5g protein; 8g fat (1g sat. fat); 34g carbohydrates; 12g fiber; 20g sugars; 140mg sodium; 269mg calcium; 2mg iron; 466mg potassium; 61mg Vitamin C; 1742IU Vitamin A

SPECIAL
OCCASION

4

A CREAMY, DELICIOUS SMOOTHIE

can turn an ordinary day into a special occasion. But they can also make a red-letter day on the calendar even more fun. Whether it's St. Patrick's Day, Halloween, or even a slumber party for a gaggle of girls, a smoothie is just what you need to get the party started. For these exciting events, don't feel confined to serving smoothies in a tall glass. Pour them into small vessels (shot glasses are perfect) or freeze in ice pop molds to add some visual pizzazz to your festivities.

VALENTINE'S CHOCOLATE-CHERRY BOMB

Makes 2 smoothies

Show your love with this luscious smoothie. The cherries
are silky sweet, and the cocoa powder adds a rich depth of
flavor, plus antioxidants to boot.

1½ CUPS MILK

1½ CUPS FROZEN CHERRIES

½ CUP PLAIN GREEK YOGURT

1 TABLESPOON UNSWEETENED
COCOA POWDER

1 TABLESPOON MAPLE SYRUP,
PLUS MORE TO TASTE

1 Add all of the ingredients
to the blender, starting with
the milk.

2 Cover and blend until smooth,
about 30 seconds.

3 Taste for sweetness, adding
more maple syrup if desired.

Nutrition per serving: 296 calories; 14g protein; 12g fat (5g sat. fat); 39g
carbohydrates; 4g fiber; 21g sugars; 163mg sodium; 325mg calcium; 2mg iron; 659mg
potassium; 27mg Vitamin C; 1884IU Vitamin A

PRETTY IN PINK SLUMBER PARTY SMOOTHIE

Makes 2 smoothies

This smoothie, bright pink in color and with just the right amount of sweet, is packed with antioxidant-rich berries. I like pomegranate juice for its ruby hue and tart taste, but the fact that it's a good source of potassium, folate, and Vitamin K doesn't hurt either.

½ CUP COCONUT MILK

¼ CUP POMEGRANATE JUICE

1½ CUPS SLICED STRAWBERRIES

1½ CUPS FROZEN RASPBERRIES

½ CUP PLAIN GREEK YOGURT

1 TABLESPOON MAPLE SYRUP, PLUS MORE TO TASTE

1. Add all of the ingredients to the blender, starting with the liquids.

2. Cover and blend until smooth, about 30 seconds.

3. Taste for sweetness, adding more maple syrup if desired.

Nutrition per serving: 234 calories; 7g protein; 9g fat (3g sat. fat); 34g carbohydrates; 10g fiber; 22g sugars; 61mg sodium; 110mg calcium; 2mg iron; 440mg potassium; 114mg Vitamin C; 1602IU Vitamin A

MINTY ST. PATTY'S SHAKE

Makes 2 smoothies

Go green on St. Patrick's Day with this sweet,
but not spinach-y, smoothie.

1½ CUPS UNSWEETENED ALMOND MILK

1 BANANA, SLICED AND FROZEN

1 CUP BABY SPINACH

1½ CUPS FROZEN GREEN GRAPES

10 MINT LEAVES

1 Add all of the ingredients to the blender, starting with the almond milk.

2 Cover and blend until smooth, about 30 seconds.

Nutrition per serving: 172 calories; 3g protein; 3g fat (0g sat. fat); 38g carbohydrates; 4g fiber; 26g sugars; 160mg sodium; 192mg calcium; 2mg iron; 583mg potassium; 26mg Vitamin C; 2325IU Vitamin A

APRIL FOOLS' DAY "MUD" SMOOTHIE

Makes 2 smoothies

Give the kids a glass of "mud" for breakfast on April Fools' Day. It may look bad, but it tastes like brownie batter. Yum! Add the pinch of salt only if your peanut butter is salt-free.

1½ CUPS UNSWEETENED ALMOND MILK

3 DATES, PREFERABLY MEDJOOL, PITTED

1½ CUPS BABY SPINACH

1½ CUPS FROZEN BLUEBERRIES

3 TABLESPOONS PEANUT BUTTER

3 TABLESPOONS UNSWEETENED COCOA POWDER

1 PINCH SALT

2 TEASPOONS AGAVE NECTAR

1. Add all of the ingredients to the blender, starting with the almond milk.

2. Cover and blend until smooth, about 30 seconds.

Nutrition per serving: 375 calories; 11g protein; 15g fat (3g sat. fat); 60g carbohydrates; 12g fiber; 42g sugars; 256mg sodium; 245mg calcium; 4mg iron; 600mg potassium; 23mg Vitamin C; 3237IU Vitamin A

CINCO DE MAYO MANGO "MARGARITA"

Makes 2 smoothies

Blend up this sweet slurp to celebrate Cinco de Mayo
with the kids. This is the only recipe that includes refined sugar;
feel free to leave it out.

2 TABLESPOONS GRANULATED SUGAR,
OPTIONAL

1½ CUPS COCONUT WATER

2 CUPS FROZEN MANGO CHUNKS

1½ TEASPOONS LIME JUICE

1. If using, place the sugar on a small plate. Wet the rims of two glasses with a damp paper towel. Place the rims on the sugar and twist to coat.

2. Add the coconut water, mango, and lime juice to the blender.

3. Cover and blend until smooth, about 30 seconds. Pour into the sugar-rimmed glasses, if using, or into glasses without a sugar rim.

Nutrition per serving: 134 calories; 3g protein; 1g fat (1g sat. fat); 32g carbohydrates; 5g fiber; 27g sugars; 190mg sodium; 62mg calcium; 1mg iron; 732mg potassium; 66mg Vitamin C; 1787IU Vitamin A

SUNNY DAY STRAWBERRY-LEMONADE SLUSHIE

Makes 2 smoothies

Coconut water may be full of electrolytes and potassium, but I like it for its light, tropical flavor. This refreshing pink drink isn't super thick, but it is perfectly sippable on a hot summer's day.

1½ CUPS COCONUT WATER

2 TABLESPOONS LEMON JUICE

1 CUP FROZEN STRAWBERRIES

1 TABLESPOON AGAVE NECTAR, PLUS MORE TO TASTE

1. Add all of the ingredients to the blender, starting with the coconut water.

2. Cover and blend until smooth, about 30 seconds.

3. Taste for sweetness, adding more agave nectar if desired.

Nutrition per serving: 92 calories; 2g protein; 1g fat (0g sat. fat); 22g carbohydrates; 4g fiber; 17g sugars; 190mg sodium; 125mg calcium; 1mg iron; 435mg potassium; 7mg Vitamin C; 334IU Vitamin A

BLOODY FANTASTIC HALLOWEEN SMOOTHIE

Makes 2 smoothies

Serve these blood-red smoothies in small glasses at a Halloween
party or freeze them in ice pop molds. Either way, everyone will enjoy
these devilishly sweet slurps.

1 CUP COLD WATER

1 CUP FRESH OR FROZEN RASPBERRIES

2 CUPS FROZEN CHERRIES

AGAVE NECTAR, OPTIONAL

1. Add the water and the raspberries to the blender.

2. Cover and blend until smooth. Strain through a fine-mesh strainer, discarding the seeds. Pour the raspberry mixture back into the blender and add the cherries.

3. Cover and blend until smooth, about 30 seconds, adding additional water if necessary.

4. Taste for sweetness, adding agave nectar if desired.

Nutrition per serving: 129 calories; 2g protein; 1g fat (0g sat. fat); 32g carbohydrates;
7g fiber; 23g sugars; 4mg sodium; 39mg calcium; 1mg iron; 436mg potassium; 27mg
Vitamin C; 119IU Vitamin A

CRANBERRY-MAPLE CHRISTMAS SMOOTHIE

Makes 2 smoothies

Give your family some sweet sustenance as they're unwrapping presents on Christmas morning. This smoothie will be a welcome gift.

1¼ CUPS UNSWEETENED ALMOND MILK

1 CUP PLAIN GREEK YOGURT

¼ CUP FRESH OR FROZEN CRANBERRIES

½ CUP FROZEN RASPBERRIES

1 TEASPOON VANILLA EXTRACT

¼ CUP MAPLE SYRUP, PLUS MORE TO TASTE

1. Add all of the ingredients to the blender, starting with the almond milk.

2. Cover and blend until smooth, about 30 seconds.

3. Taste for sweetness, adding more maple syrup if desired.

Nutrition per serving: 326 calories; 10g protein; 17g fat (5g sat. fat); 37g carbohydrates; 5g fiber; 26g sugars; 243mg sodium; 256mg calcium; 2mg iron; 283mg potassium; 44mg Vitamin C; 3256IU Vitamin A

FIGGY PUDDING CHRISTMAS SMOOTHIE

Makes 2 smoothies

This thick and creamy smoothie has a warm, toasty flavor thanks to the cinnamon, and a pleasant tartness courtesy of the cranberries. Feel free to use canned pears if a ripe pear isn't available.

1½ CUPS MILK

½ CUP FRESH OR FROZEN CRANBERRIES

4 DRIED MISSION FIGS, CHOPPED

1 RIPE PEAR, CORED AND CHOPPED

¼ TEASPOON GROUND CINNAMON

1 PINCH GROUND ALLSPICE

HONEY, OPTIONAL

1. Add the milk, cranberries, figs, pear, cinnamon, and allspice to the blender, starting with the milk.

2. Cover and blend until smooth, about 30 seconds.

3. Taste for sweetness, adding honey if desired.

Nutrition per serving: 211 calories; 8g protein; 4g fat (2g sat. fat); 38g carbohydrates; 6g fiber; 18g sugars; 113mg sodium; 308mg calcium; 1mg iron; 583mg potassium; 9mg Vitamin C; 417IU Vitamin A

JANUARY 2ND SMOOTHIE

Makes 2 smoothies

After New Year's Day I am ready for some serious detox. This lightly sweetened, veggie-packed smoothie hits all the right notes and, thanks to its beautiful green color and creamy texture, I never feel like I'm depriving myself.

1 CUP COCONUT MILK

1 RIPE AVOCADO, CUT INTO CHUNKS

1 CUP CHOPPED CUCUMBER

1 CUP BABY SPINACH

1 CUP FROZEN PINEAPPLE CHUNKS

1 TEASPOON AGAVE NECTAR, PLUS MORE TO TASTE

1. Add all of the ingredients to the blender, starting with the coconut milk.

2. Cover and blend until smooth, about 30 seconds.

3. Taste for sweetness, adding more agave nectar if desired.

Nutrition per serving: 261 calories; 3g protein; 17g fat (4g sat. fat); 29g carbohydrates; 9g fiber; 16g sugars; 38mg sodium; 108mg calcium; 2mg iron; 699mg potassium; 59mg Vitamin C; 2333IU Vitamin A

WHOLE-
FOOD
JUICES

5

One of smoothies' key selling points is that since they are made from whole fruits and vegetables, their natural sugars are partnered with fiber, making for a filling, healthy drink. Traditional juices, on the other hand, while vitamin and mineral-rich, are low in fiber, making them a good shot of nutrients but not necessarily nourishing. The juices in this chapter are different. Blending whole fruits retains all of their health benefits, including their fiber. These drinks have more body than traditional juices, but also tons of flavor. For the tastiest results start with cold fruit.

IT'S LIKE DRINKING A PIECE OF SWEET, JUICY FRUIT.

GROOVY GRAPEFRUIT

Makes 2 juices

This pretty pink juice is like a grapefruit distilled to its essence:
bracing, sweet, and tart all at the same time. To me,
Groovy Grapefruit is perfect without extra sweetness, but little
ones might appreciate some agave action.

2 PINK GRAPEFRUITS, PEELED AND SEEDED

6 CHUNKS FROZEN PINEAPPLE (ABOUT ¼ CUP)

AGAVE NECTAR, OPTIONAL

1. Add the grapefruit and frozen pineapple to a blender.

2. Cover and blend until smooth and frothy, about 30 seconds.

3. Taste for sweetness, adding agave nectar if desired.

Nutrition per serving: 114 calories; 2g protein; 0g fat (0g sat. fat); 29g carbohydrates; 4g fiber; 19g sugars; 0mg sodium; 57mg calcium; 0mg iron; 355mg potassium; 86mg Vitamin C; 2841IU Vitamin A

STRAWBERRY-COCO COOLER

Makes 2 juices

This bright pink juice is delicious any time of year. But for that fresh, summer-in-a-glass taste, buy ripe strawberries from your local farmer's market in May or June. Sweet and delicate, these ruby red fruits make for a sublime juice. Don't be surprised to see small, strawberry-stained mouths begging for more.

1¼ CUPS COCONUT WATER

1 CUP SLICED STRAWBERRIES

4 FROZEN STRAWBERRIES

2 MINT LEAVES

AGAVE NECTAR, OPTIONAL

1. Add the coconut water, strawberries, and mint leaves to the blender, starting with the coconut water.

2. Cover and blend until smooth and frothy, about 30 seconds.

3. Taste for sweetness, adding agave nectar if desired.

Nutrition per serving: 60 calories; 2g protein; 1g fat (0g sat. fat); 13g carbohydrates; 4g fiber; 9g sugars; 158mg sodium; 52mg calcium; 1mg iron; 528mg potassium; 62mg Vitamin C; 12IU Vitamin A

TOTALLY TANGERINE

Makes 2 juices

This dazzling orange juice is sensational, and it boasts a flavor as intense as its color. The mango adds some chill and body to the juice, but feel free to leave it out. Look for tangerines the size of tennis balls.

2 MEDIUM TANGERINES, PEELED AND SEEDED

10 CHUNKS FROZEN MANGO (ABOUT ½ CUP)

1. Add the tangerines and mango to the blender.

2. Cover and blend until smooth and frothy, about 30 seconds.

Nutrition per serving: 71 calories; 1g protein; 0g fat (0g sat. fat); 18g carbohydrates; 2g fiber; 15g sugars; 2mg sodium; 37mg calcium; 0mg iron; 215mg potassium; 38mg Vitamin C; 1046IU Vitamin A

KIWI SLUSH

Makes 2 juices

Kiwi is perfect for whole fruit juicing. It's packed with water, and its flesh virtually disappears in the blender. A touch of agave makes this juice sing, but taste the smoothie first since the sweetness depends entirely on the ripeness of the kiwis.

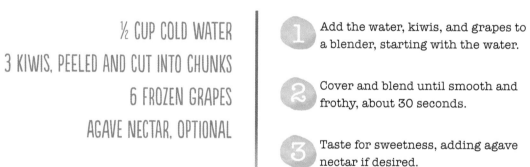

½ CUP COLD WATER

3 KIWIS, PEELED AND CUT INTO CHUNKS

6 FROZEN GRAPES

AGAVE NECTAR, OPTIONAL

1 Add the water, kiwis, and grapes to a blender, starting with the water.

2 Cover and blend until smooth and frothy, about 30 seconds.

3 Taste for sweetness, adding agave nectar if desired.

Nutrition per serving: 68 calories; 1g protein; 1g fat (0g sat. fat); 16g carbohydrates; 3g fiber; 11g sugars; 0mg sodium; 38mg calcium; 0mg iron; 337mg potassium; 96mg Vitamin C; 97IU Vitamin A

WATERMELON JUICE

Makes 2 juices

This juice bursts with the flavor of summer; it's just plain yummy.
Since it's swollen with water, watermelon blends like a dream.
Watermelon is also packed with lycopene, a phytonutrient that boosts
heart and bone health—important for kids of all ages.

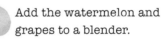

3 CUPS CUBED WATERMELON

4 FROZEN GRAPES

1 Add the watermelon and grapes to a blender.

2 Cover and blend until smooth and frothy, about 30 seconds.

Nutrition per serving: 71 calories; 1g protein; 0g fat (0g sat. fat); 18g carbohydrates; 1g fiber; 15g sugars; 2mg sodium; 17mg calcium; 1mg iron; 265mg potassium; 19mg Vitamin C; 1302IU Vitamin A

BERRY GOOD JUICE

Makes 2 juices

Fresh berries are a summertime delight, and this sweet juice
makes the most of their delectable flavor. Make sure to push the juice
through a strainer to get rid of the berries' pesky seeds.

1 CUP COCONUT WATER

½ CUP BLACKBERRIES

1 CUP RASPBERRIES

1 TEASPOON AGAVE NECTAR,
PLUS MORE TO TASTE

1 Add all of the ingredients to the blender, starting with the coconut water.

2 Cover and blend until smooth, about 30 seconds. Strain the juice through a fine-mesh strainer, using a spoon to push through as much of the solids as possible.

3 Taste for sweetness, adding more agave nectar if desired.

Nutrition per serving: 80 calories; 2g protein; 1g fat (0g sat. fat); 18g carbohydrates; 7g fiber; 10g sugars; 127mg sodium; 55mg calcium; 1mg iron; 451mg potassium; 26mg Vitamin C; 97IU Vitamin A

MANGO JUICE

makes 2 juices

Blend up this juice and be ready for a pop of super mango flavor. Just remember: The riper the mango, the sweeter the drink.

¾ CUP COCONUT WATER

1 CUP CHOPPED MANGO (ABOUT 1 MEDIUM)

6 CHUNKS FROZEN PINEAPPLE (ABOUT ¼ CUP)

AGAVE NECTAR, OPTIONAL

1 Add the coconut water, mango, and pineapple to the blender, starting with the coconut water.

2 Cover and blend until smooth and frothy, about 30 seconds.

3 Taste for sweetness, adding agave nectar if desired.

Nutrition per serving: 87 calories; 2g protein; 1g fat (0g sat. fat); 21g carbohydrates; 3g fiber; 18g sugars; 96mg sodium; 36mg calcium; 1mg iron; 409mg potassium; 87mg Vitamin C; 917IU Vitamin A

PINEAPPLE PERFECT

Makes 2 juices

Tangy and sweet, this juice has a bit of body. Feel free to add a
splash more water if you want a thinner sip.

½ CUP COLD WATER

2 CUPS CHOPPED PINEAPPLE

4 MINT LEAVES

1. Add all of the ingredients to the blender, starting with the water.

2. Cover and blend until smooth and frothy, about 30 seconds.

Nutrition per serving: 83 calories; 1g protein; 0g fat (0g sat. fat); 22g carbohydrates;
2g fiber; 16g sugars; 3mg sodium; 23mg calcium; 0mg iron; 180mg potassium; 79mg
Vitamin C; 96IU Vitamin A

HONEYDEW-CUCUMBER JUICE

Makes 2 juices

Water-rich honeydew and cucumber are ideal for whole fruit juicing.
I love the slight bracing quality the cucumber brings to the drink,
and I can't help thinking a drop of gin would be simply delicious . . .
after the kids are in bed, of course.

2½ CUPS HONEYDEW MELON CHUNKS
½ CUP ENGLISH CUCUMBER CHUNKS
AGAVE NECTAR, OPTIONAL

1. Add the melon and cucumber to the blender.

2. Cover and blend until smooth and frothy, about 30 seconds.

3. Taste for sweetness, adding agave nectar if desired.

nutrition per serving: 80 calories; 1g protein; 0g fat (0g sat. fat); 20g carbohydrates; 2g fiber; 18g sugars; 39mg sodium; 17mg calcium; 0mg iron; 523mg potassium; 39mg Vitamin C; 134IU Vitamin A

STRAWBERRY-WATERMELON AGUA FRESCA

Makes 2 juices

I distinctly remember tasting cilantro for the first time as a preteen (at Chili's!) and thinking that the restaurant hadn't washed the soap off its dishes. I avoided the leafy herb for many years before deciding that I liked Mexican food too much to shun cilantro forever. After years of rigorous training I am now a superfan. But if you're not, substitute basil or mint, or just leave it out altogether.

2 CUPS WATERMELON CUBES

½ CUP SLICED STRAWBERRIES

½ TEASPOON LIME JUICE

4 SPRIGS CILANTRO

AGAVE NECTAR, TO TASTE

1. Add the watermelon, strawberries, lime juice, and cilantro to the blender.

2. Cover and blend until smooth and frothy, about 30 seconds.

3. Taste for sweetness, adding agave nectar if desired.

Nutrition per serving: 58 calories; 1g protein; 0g fat (0g sat. fat); 15g carbohydrates; 1g fiber; 11g sugars; 2mg sodium; 17mg calcium; 1mg iron; 230mg potassium; 35mg Vitamin C; 870IU Vitamin A

CHERRY-VANILLA SODA

Makes 2 juices

There is something about the combination of cherry and
vanilla that makes kids go gaga.

¼ CUP COLD WATER

½ CUP FROZEN CHERRIES

½ TEASPOON VANILLA EXTRACT

1 TABLESPOON AGAVE NECTAR

1½ CUPS CLUB SODA

1. Add the water, cherries, vanilla, and agave to the blender.

2. Cover and blend until smooth and frothy, about 30 seconds.

3. Pour the cherry juice into two glasses. Divide the club soda evenly between the glasses and stir to combine.

Nutrition per serving: 54 calories; 0g protein; 0g fat (0g sat. fat); 14g carbohydrates; 1g fiber; 13g sugars; 37mg sodium; 14mg calcium; 0mg iron; 89mg potassium; 3mg Vitamin C; 25IU Vitamin A

CANTALOUPE-BLACKBERRY BREEZE JUICE

Makes 2 juices

The cantaloupe flavor really shines through in this thick juice.

½ CUP COLD WATER

1 CUP BLACKBERRIES

1½ CUPS CHOPPED CANTALOUPE

1. Add the water and blackberries to the blender.

2. Cover and blend until smooth, about 30 seconds.

3. Strain the juice through a fine-mesh strainer, using a spoon to push through as many of the solids as possible.

4. Return the blackberry juice to the blender. Add the cantaloupe, cover, and blend until smooth and frothy, about 30 seconds.

Nutrition per serving: 72 calories; 2g protein; 1g fat (0g sat. fat); 17g carbohydrates; 5g fiber; 13g sugars; 20mg sodium; 32mg calcium; 1mg iron; 437mg potassium; 60mg Vitamin C; 4212IU Vitamin A

TREATS

6

WHILE ANY SMOOTHIE CAN FEEL LIKE A TREAT, SOMETIMES A TRUE,

honest-to-goodness *treat* is required. That's where these smoothies—let's just call them shakes—come in. Made with real fruit, milk, and cold, creamy frozen yogurt, sorbet, or gelato, these are not your everyday sips. Because these aren't made with ice cream they are even a tiny bit virtuous, but of course feel free to use regular ice cream if a capital letter TREAT is in order.

NUTELLA-BANANA CREAM

Makes 2 shakes

These spectacular shakes are so thick they're
almost spoon-able.

1 CUP UNSWEETENED ALMOND MILK

2 BANANAS, SLICED AND FROZEN

2 TABLESPOONS NUTELLA

1 Add all of the ingredients to
the blender, starting with the
almond milk.

2 Cover and blend until smooth,
about 30 seconds.

Nutrition per serving: 225 calories; 3g protein; 7g fat (2g sat. fat); 39g carbohydrates;
4g fiber; 14g sugars; 99mg sodium; 126mg calcium; 1mg iron; 517mg potassium; 10mg
Vitamin C; 326IU Vitamin A

COCONUT-BLACKBERRY SHAKE

Makes 2 shakes

This dessert smoothie is delish with regular cow's milk, but something special when you blend it up with coconut milk. Whichever you choose, the blackberries are the star of the show.

⅔ CUP COCONUT MILK

1 CUP BLACKBERRIES

1½ CUPS VANILLA FROZEN YOGURT

1 Add the coconut milk and blackberries to the blender.

2 Cover and blend until smooth, about 30 seconds.

3 Add the frozen yogurt, cover, and blend again until just combined.

Nutrition per serving: 226 calories; 5g protein; 8g fat (5g sat. fat); 36g carbohydrates; 4g fiber; 32g sugars; 100mg sodium; 206mg calcium; 1mg iron; 375mg potassium; 16mg Vitamin C; 550IU Vitamin A

ALMOND-DREAM DATE

Makes 2 shakes

Make a date with almonds and whip up this sweet shake. It is also divine made with chocolate frozen yogurt. If you're using fresh fruit (not frozen) in your smoothie treat, be sure to blend the fruit and milk together, then simply pulse in the frozen yogurt or sorbet. If you blend it all together at once the shake might become too thin.

1 CUP UNSWEETENED ALMOND MILK

4 DATES, PREFERABLY MEDJOOL, PITTED

2 TABLESPOONS ALMOND BUTTER

1½ CUPS VANILLA FROZEN YOGURT

1 Add the almond milk, dates, and almond butter to the blender.

2 Cover and blend until smooth, about 30 seconds.

3 Add the frozen yogurt, cover, and blend again until just combined.

Nutrition per serving: 423 calories; 9g protein; 17g fat (4g sat. fat); 66g carbohydrates; 5g fiber; 58g sugars; 185mg sodium; 341mg calcium; 1mg iron; 777mg potassium; 1mg Vitamin C; 551IU Vitamin A

PINEAPPLE-MANGO TANGO

Makes 2 shakes

A brilliant bright orange, this tropical-tasting smoothie hits the spot on a steamy day, but I like it even more when the weather is at its chilly worst. Just close your eyes, sip, and enjoy a relaxing vacation . . . at least until you've devoured the last drop.

¾ CUP ORANGE JUICE
¾ CUP COCONUT MILK
1 CUP MANGO SORBET
⅔ CUP FROZEN PINEAPPLE CHUNKS

1. Add all of the ingredients to the blender, starting with the liquids.

2. Cover and blend until smooth, about 30 seconds.

Nutrition per serving: 211 calories; 1g protein; 2g fat (2g sat. fat); 50g carbohydrates; 2g fiber; 43g sugars; 8mg sodium; 47mg calcium; 1mg iron; 133mg potassium; 58mg Vitamin C; 760IU Vitamin A

STRAWBERRIES AND CREAM

Makes 2 shakes

This super-strawberry shake is a guaranteed kid-pleaser. High in Vitamin C and relatively low in calories thanks to the sorbet, it's one treat you can feel extra-good about.

¾ CUP COCONUT MILK

2 CUPS SLICED STRAWBERRIES

1½ TEASPOONS VANILLA EXTRACT

1 CUP STRAWBERRY SORBET

1. Add the coconut milk, strawberries, and vanilla to the blender.

2. Cover and blend until smooth, about 30 seconds.

3. Add the sorbet, cover, and blend again until just combined.

Nutrition per serving: 209 calories; 1g protein; 2g fat (2g sat. fat); 47g carbohydrates; 5g fiber; 39g sugars; 7mg sodium; 64mg calcium; 1mg iron; 288mg potassium; 110mg Vitamin C; 207IU Vitamin A

CREAMY AVOCADO INDULGENCE

Makes 2 shakes

This out-of-this-world shake may be the creamiest drink in the entire book. Ultra-smooth, it tastes just barely of avocado and is 100 percent amazing. Aside from being delicious, this treat is also a looker: It's a gorgeous, seafoam green color. You could sub in coconut sorbet for less fat and calories, but I am addicted to Talenti's sublime Caribbean Coconut gelato.

½ CUP COCONUT MILK

1 CUP COCONUT GELATO

1 RIPE AVOCADO, CUT INTO CHUNKS

1 TEASPOON LIME JUICE

1. Add all of the ingredients to the blender, starting with the coconut milk.

2. Cover and blend until smooth, about 30 seconds.

Nutrition per serving: 379 calories; 6g protein; 25g fat (10g sat. fat); 36g carbohydrates; 7g fiber; 28g sugars; 50mg sodium; 187mg calcium; 1mg iron; 513mg potassium; 10mg Vitamin C; 573IU Vitamin A

CINNAMON-CARAMEL APPLE

Makes 2 shakes

This creamy shake tastes much more decadent than it actually is.
While the flavors may be a natural fit for fall, I promise it will be
well-received any time of year.

½ CUP MILK

1 APPLE, CORED AND CHOPPED

¼ TEASPOON GROUND CINNAMON

1¼ CUPS CARAMEL FROZEN YOGURT

1. Add the milk, apple, and cinnamon to the blender, starting with the milk.

2. Cover and blend until smooth, about 30 seconds.

3. Add the frozen yogurt, cover, and blend again until just combined.

Nutrition per serving: 201 calories; 6g protein; 5g fat (3g sat. fat); 35g carbohydrates; 2g fiber; 28g sugars; 100mg sodium; 188mg calcium; 1mg iron; 332mg potassium; 4mg Vitamin C; 353IU Vitamin A

DAD'S CEREAL SHAKE

Makes 2 shakes

I inherited a love of cereal from my dad. One of his
signature breakfast moves was mixing two (or even three!) cereals
together, a culinary innovation I found revolutionary as a kid.
My dad came up with this recipe, and as far as I'm concerned his
tastes are still spot-on.

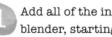

1 CUP MILK

1½ BANANAS, SLICED AND FROZEN

½ CUP GRANOLA

½ CUP CRACKLIN' OAT BRAN CEREAL

1 TABLESPOON CHOCOLATE SYRUP

1. Add all of the ingredients to the blender, starting with the milk.

2. Cover and blend until smooth, about 30 seconds.

Nutrition per serving: 400 calories; 12g protein; 13g fat (4g sat. fat); 63g
carbohydrates; 8g fiber; 27g sugars; 65mg sodium; 140mg calcium; 3mg iron; 805mg
potassium; 15mg Vitamin C; 465IU Vitamin A

CHERRY-CHOCOLATE EGGNOG

Makes 2 shakes

My husband is one of my best taste testers. He sips, and I await his verdict. When Dave first tasted this rich shake, he was strangely quiet and then asked me what was in it. After I responded he said, "Well, how could it not be good?" Exactly.

1 CUP EGGNOG
½ CUP FROZEN CHERRIES
1 CUP CHOCOLATE FROZEN YOGURT

1. Add the eggnog and cherries to the blender.

2. Cover and blend until smooth, about 30 seconds.

3. Add the frozen yogurt, cover, and blend again until just combined.

Nutrition per serving: 275 calories; 8g protein; 6g fat (5g sat. fat); 47g carbohydrates; 3g fiber; 44g sugars; 185mg sodium; 292mg calcium; 1mg iron; 529mg potassium; 3mg Vitamin C; 547IU Vitamin A

PIÑA COLADA SHAKE

Makes 2 shakes

It may be a cliché, but to me nothing says "I'm on holiday"
like a piña colada. Let the kids in on the fun with this utterly
transporting tropical drink.

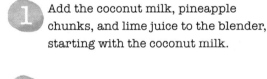

1¼ CUPS COCONUT MILK

1 CUP FROZEN PINEAPPLE CHUNKS

1 TEASPOON LIME JUICE

1 CUP COCONUT GELATO

1 Add the coconut milk, pineapple chunks, and lime juice to the blender, starting with the coconut milk.

2 Cover and blend until smooth, about 30 seconds.

3 Add the gelato, cover, and blend again until just combined.

Nutrition per serving: 285 calories; 4g protein; 12g fat (9g sat. fat); 41g carbohydrates; 2g fiber; 37g sugars; 50mg sodium; 224mg calcium; 1mg iron; 149mg potassium; 40mg Vitamin C; 662IU Vitamin A

BANANA-BLUEBERRY CRUNCH

Makes 2 shakes

When choosing a granola for this berry-purple shake,
I prefer one with just oats and nuts. Raisins or other dried fruit
will make for a chunkier sip.

⅔ CUP UNSWEETENED ALMOND MILK

1 BANANA, SLICED AND FROZEN

1 CUP BLUEBERRIES

1 CUP VANILLA FROZEN YOGURT

¼ CUP GRANOLA

1 Add all of the ingredients to the blender, starting with the almond milk.

2 Cover and blend until smooth, about 30 seconds.

Nutrition per serving: 296 calories; 7g protein; 9g fat (3g sat. fat); 50g carbohydrates; 5g fiber; 35g sugars; 127mg sodium; 189mg calcium; 1mg iron; 565mg potassium; 12mg Vitamin C; 399IU Vitamin A

ACKNOWLEDGMENTS

First and foremost, thank you to Sharon Bowers. You started me on this journey, and I am so grateful.

Thank you to my wonderful editor Adam Kowit for being as excited about smoothies as I am. My gratitude extends to the entire team at Houghton Mifflin Harcourt including Rebecca Liss, Brittany Edwards, Brad Parsons, Jessica Gilo, Molly Aronica, Melissa Lotfy, Alissa Faden, Helen Seachrist, and Kevin Watt.

Thank you to Natalia Stasenko, MS, RD for your nutritional advice and analysis. I could always count on you for thoughtful answers to my numerous questions.

The *Smoothie-licious* photo team was top-notch. Huge thank yous to Lauren Volo for your beautiful photos, Mariana Velasquez for making all of the smoothies look so delicious, and Alix Winsby for bringing just the right combination of playfulness and sophistication to the table.

This book would be a shadow of itself without my enthusiastic testers. Tara Bench, you were a lifesaver! I am also incredibly grateful to Jean Wilkie, Jan Henderson, and Linda Kennedy. Thank you also to Sara Woods and the lovely Audrey Bellezza. And much love to Heather Date for your taste-testing and fervent support of the book (and me).

Thank you, always, to Danielle Wilkie, Allison Graham, Felicity Rowe, Nicole Page, and Jessica Winchell Morsa.

My gratitude goes to my colleagues at *Parents*, Steve Engel and Heidi Reavis, and all of my Rosaberry chefs and clients, especially Lauren Slayton of Foodtrainers for your years of support.

My parents dove into this project with wholehearted enthusiasm. They tried out recipes, recruited testers, and even concocted new smoothies from scratch. Mom and Dad—you're the best. I also send my love to David, China, Cole, and Tasha.

Finally, thank you to Dave and Rosa. You gamely ignored the non-stop blender whirring, happily tried smoothie variations all day long, and never admitted to being tired of a liquid diet. I look forward to drinking smoothies with you both for many happy years to come.

INDEX